Confessions of an Ex-Bachelor

Also by William July II

Brothers, Lust, and Love

The Hidden Lover

Understanding the Tin Man

William July II

Confessions
of an
Ex-Bachelor

*How to Sift Through All
the Game Players to
Find Mr. Right*

BROADWAY BOOKS
NEW YORK

BROADWAY

PRINTED IN THE UNITED STATES OF AMERICA

BROADWAY BOOKS and its logo, a letter B bisected on the diagonal, are trademarks of Random House, Inc.

Visit our website at www.broadwaybooks.com

First edition published 2003

Book design by Jennifer Ann Daddio

Library of Congress Cataloging-in-Publication Data
July, William.
    Confessions of an ex-bachelor : how to sift through all the game players to find Mr. Right / William July II.— 1st ed.
        p.   cm.
    1. Bachelors—Psychology.   2. Man-woman relationships.   I. Title.
HQ800.3.J85 2003
306.7—dc21
                                                    2003050245

ISBN 0-7679-1107-5

1   3   5   7   9   10   8   6   4   2

Dedicated to those who seek
sacred companionship

*A man will leave his father and mother
and be united to his wife,
and the two will become one flesh.*

—EPHESIANS 5:31

*A wife of noble character who can find?
She is worth far more than rubies.*

—PROVERBS 31:10

Acknowledgments

First, I give thanks to God. It is God who powers my words.

I've come a long way since the hot summer of 1996 when my first book was published. I've gone from selling books from the trunk of my car to being given the red-carpet treatment when lecturing before hundreds and selling out boxes of books. Thank you to every person who has bought my books. You keep me in print. My success and my gratitude comes from the bottom of my heart.

Thanks to my wife for her continued support. What a flight our life has been. I'm glad you're my copilot.

A huge thanks to my parents. I could never say or do enough to repay them for their endless support, encouragement, and teachings.

Much appreciation goes out to the "think tank," the

men and women who answer my surveys online or fill out the questionnaires at my lectures and seminars. Keep those candid comments coming.

Applause for the Doubleday team. Everyone there, from the mailroom staff to the publisher, has made my literary career a dream come true in a better way than I ever imagined.

A super thanks to my editor, the incomparable Janet Hill. I can't say enough about how important it is to have the right editor. Janet is solid gold.

A pat on the back to my agent, Jeff Herman, for being an agent who's unlike any other I've ever met.

Contents

Introduction

The relationship world for singles is sometimes compared metaphorically to a jungle. It's a place filled with a variety of species, plus mystery, adventure, beauty, and dangers—both hidden and apparent. That analogy becomes even more realistic when one considers the issues faced by those women who desire to date men who have matrimony on their minds.

But in writing this book, it wasn't my intent to imply that all women necessarily want to get married or even need to be married. Rather, this book is a response to the droves of women I encounter who do want to be married and have grown tired of the game players and swinging bachelor types who don't want the same thing. They want directions on how to steer clear of the players and sift through the available men to find the men who, like them, want to be married.

That's where *Confessions of an Ex-Bachelor* comes in. This book is a clear road map for single women who want a husband, to learn how to identify and steer clear of game players while looking more successfully for the right types. While I can't guarantee that every woman reading this book will never again be played by a player or that she'll go out and meet Mr. Right, I can guarantee that she'll be much more empowered in the romantic marketplace.

No one is better qualified to tell women about the mind-set and games of bachelors than an ex-bachelor. I say that because you can't really trust many active bachelors to be 100 percent forthright; they're still in the game. This type of book is best written in hindsight, which is, after all, 20/20. So, from your questions to me, I find myself, after five years of marriage, reflecting on bachelorhood.

I've been called a playa hata by some guys for admitting these things so openly. One male radio host flat out said to me, "Man, stop giving away all of our secrets to the women." But that's exactly the mentality I'm trying to help us all overcome. We've got to overcome this feeling that love and relationships are a game, because it isn't doing anyone any good.

As I've written in *Understanding the Tin Man*, bachelorhood is a sacred ground to men, a place they reach and don't want to surrender until they've had every drop of its sweet nectar. To help you understand this, I've gone a step further in this book and defined bachelorhood in three distinct stages. This will help you understand the mind of the bachelor so you'll be better able to understand, communicate with, and, ultimately, sift through the game players to find the serious men.

This book can be trusted as a map because it's written by a former general in the Bachelor Corps. This book openly reveals the secrets, the games, and the mind-set of bachelors to women who want the straight truth. Pardon my directness. But it's the only way to tell the truth. So get ready to hear me tell it in a way that nobody else will.

Confessions of an Ex-Bachelor

1

Why Buy the Cow When You Can Get the Milk for Free?

The truth is simple, but it may not sound so good. The fact of the matter is that a man doesn't have to get married to have the comforts of being married. He can have sex. He can have companionship. He can have loyalty. He can have financial sharing or support. He can have children. Truth be told, he can have anything that a married man can get without making the commitment. This is especially true if he's a highly desirable man who knows how to play a good Don Juan act. What's happening is that men are realizing they can have everything without making a commitment, and that's exactly what some of them are doing. Marriage has become mainly an issue of responsibility and accountability, or lack thereof, for the man.

Limited Responsibility and Accountability

I really enjoyed the film *Love and Basketball*, and it perfectly illustrates a point about men not learning to be accountable for their own feelings and actions in a relationship. There was a climactic scene (no, not the strip-poker-style one-on-one game!) in which Monica challenged Q to a game of one-on-one for his heart. This challenge was her attempt to win Q's heart two weeks before his scheduled marriage to another woman. Excuse me? This is after he absolutely dissed her in college, selfishly put his needs above hers, and then cheated on her and flaunted this fact right in her face in an attempt to hurt her feelings.

Yet Monica had enough love left in her heart for Q to challenge him to this game. In the film, the challenge worked and Monica won Q back. But in real life, it's not so simple. In real life, a man has to make some serious and significant changes after the type of rift Monica and Q had before he can be a man capable of making a real commitment and sticking to it. In reality, if this man didn't make a significant change in character and attitude, the marriage would be doomed to drama and divorce. In real life, one would have to ask, "Did he really change? How and why?" Unfortunately, men who don't learn to be accountable for their actions in relationships don't just magically get it by the next scene in time for the happy ending.

Yet relationships like Monica and Q's play out daily in the real world as well. Every day women are allowing men to do things they should be held accountable for in relationships but aren't. What's most alarming is hearing some of the excuses women make for these guys in their attempt to rationalize why they are remaining in a relationship with them. For example, Melody was living with Brian, whom she was going to marry. When she discovered she was pregnant, at the same time she discovered that Brian was cheating on her. To make matters worse, she learned that he had been cheating for quite a while and that the other woman was also pregnant. Their children were born only a few months apart. All this time Brian continued living with Melody. Eventually he decided he didn't want the relationship and left her, only to return months later wanting to move back in. Now Melody's wondering if he has changed and if she should give him another chance.

Melody and Brian's story is a perfect example of limited male responsibility and accountability. Melody is delusional to think Brian is in love with her. Moreover, he's not even acting responsibly toward her or their child. However, since Melody's got it fixed in her mind that he's the one for her, she's not reading the obvious facts in this terrible situation and is still asking for more.

Another example is Tonya and Darrell's so-called relationship, which occurred mainly within the four walls of her bedroom during the hours of 11 P.M. and 2 A.M. She knew he was seeing another woman in a nearby city because he had told her. But he complained to Tonya that his current girlfriend was too demanding and he was going to stop seeing her. Tonya wrote to ask me if I thought he would eventually stop seeing the other woman or if she was a fool for believing him. She even went on to say that she knew she was being foolish but she really loved this man and wanted to get him for her own.

Here's the real deal. If Tonya "gets" Darrell from the other woman, she won't have him anyway. Darrell has two women in two cities (that we know of) and he is getting all the sex, love, and attention he could ever want without being accountable or taking responsibility. This type of man isn't going to change. He doesn't have to because he's a single man with no accountability to the woman or the relationship. When given such an opportunity, it takes a man of high character not to take advantage of the situation. Some men won't take advantage, but if you keep wearing a sign that says "I'm available on your terms," even a good man may start to use you.

HEAR NO EVIL, SEE NO EVIL, SPEAK NO EVIL

Why do women let men get away with limited to no responsibility and accountability? In a word, denial. Many women fall into this category when it comes to the way they respond to improperly behaving men. They simply live in denial of the obvious fact that they are in a relationship that's headed for a crash. He can be caught lying over and over, but she fixes the lies in her mind. He can be caught with evidence that he's cheating, but she pretends she doesn't see it. He can even be caught with another woman and explain his way out of that too. Eddie Murphy once joked about a man whose girlfriend caught him cheating. I'll paraphrase what the man said to his girlfriend: "You didn't see me. That wasn't me. It wasn't me . . . okay, it was me. But we weren't making love. We were just having sex. I was only having sex with her." His humor pointed out the very real fact that men actually can pull off some really unbelievable stunts in relationships because some women want to be in denial for what they think is the sake of peace and stability, but it's a shaky peace and a costly stability at best.

How Bachelors Play Women

How do men get away with all this playing? Playing women doesn't require diabolical schemes or plots. These men just use some proven methods that work. More of this will be revealed later in the book, but for now, here's a primer on how bachelors play women.

UNAVAILABILITY

Unavailability is a simple technique where the man is never available unless its convenient to him. Typically this means a man will be available only when he wants sex. It sounds like too obvious of a pattern but it works, particulary if the man is a good conversationalist and can convince a woman that he really is that busy at work, or whatever his excuse for disappearing is.

DANGLING THE CARROT

In the dangling-the-carrot technique, the man always keeps the possibility of a relationship alive as a means of getting what he wants. In this method, a man intentionally gives the impression that he's always just on the verge of making a commitment. That way he can keep a woman focusing her attention on him and meeting his needs in a relationship without ever having to actually commit.

LIES, LIES, AND MORE LIES

Some men don't use subtle techniques. Instead, they just lie. I once knew a guy who said that he just outright lied to women, literally telling them whatever they wanted to hear. He was a chameleon and it was working; I'd seen him with lots of different women and each seemed to be crazy about him. This is a dangerous situation because the relationship is built on deception. It's bound to come crashing down, and when it does, it often involves many innocent bystanders.

PROVOKING FEAR

Provoking fear is the most sinister of the techniques, but some players use it. In this method, a man identifies a strong need a woman has and fills that need. For some women, it may be the need for companionship to fight loneliness, the need for the attention, the need for emotional security, or even the need for financial support. After becoming the woman's source for this need, the man then gains control over her simply by the implicit threat of removing his support. For more on this issue, refer to Chapter 6, "How to Read a Bachelor."

King Solomon Syndrome

Bachelor players are pros at manipulating women. As a result, they usually have a harem. This is what is often referred to as a little black book. But I don't think that term does it full justice. It's more like a harem of beautiful women dancing for the king, each vying for his attention and hoping to be his wife.

The harem illustrates a major principle that bachelor players operate by: the idea that there is always a woman available. If one woman isn't available, another one will be. That's how they can bounce from woman to woman like a honey bee pollinating flowers.

One of the rules given in the book *The Rules* tells women not to accept last-minute dates. While I don't really endorse that book, because it teaches women to try to deceive men into marriage, I do understand the principle behind that rule. The idea is that a man who can just call up a woman and get a date with her anytime won't appreciate and respect her as much as a woman he has to plan for. I must agree with that in principle. However, I think women shouldn't make a hard-and-fast rule about not being available for last-minute dates. Life today isn't so simple that one can't be open to spur-of-the-moment dates.

Harems are an egocentric idea. They provide the bachelor player with a variety of different women to interact with, depending on his mood and tastes at the time. Some of the types of women commonly found in a bachelor's harem are described in the next sections.

THE HOTTY

The hotty's job in the harem is to be an ego booster. The bachelor takes the hotty out to be seen with her when he wants people to admire him for whom he has on his arm. Her appearance makes him feel strong and powerful, for surely, he feels, if she's with me, I must be "the man." She has the look and she knows it. Because of her looks, she's been spoiled by many men, and she doesn't mind letting a man know that he'd better pull out his credit card and rolls of cash on dates with her.

THE NICE GIRL

The nice girl is the one he takes home to mom. He calls up the nice girl when he wants to go to church or have a wholesome picnic in the park. Her role is to be sweet, uncomplicated, and easy to please. She's also a retreat when he wants to get away from the hotty and her game-playing. Or when he desires a contrast from the carnal role of the bedroom buddy.

THE BEDROOM BUDDY

This woman is always available for sex, no questions asked. She's the woman at the other end of those late-night phone calls. She knows the guy she's dealing with is a player and doesn't care because she's playing the same game too. Like him, she just wants easy, no-hassles sex.

THE GAL PAL

She's a good friend. He confides in her. More than the other women, she hears his most intimate thoughts. She in essence provides the intimacy he desires, but doesn't place the demands on him that he would have in a relationship. His relationship with the gal pal allows him to have a safe, intimate connection with a woman while pursuing exclusively sexual relationships with the others. This allows him to have the security of always having a female ally who will be there after his flavor-of-the-month flings are over.

For more about the gal pal, refer to Chapter 5, "What Does It Take for a Bachelor to Want to Become a Groom?"

THE OUT-OF-TOWNER

This is a mainstay of the more accomplished bachelor players. The out-of-town girlfriend, using the term "girlfriend" very loosely, is the one he can fly in to see for a hot weekend. Or when she's in town, he can have some fun with her and then she's back out again. Women, beware; while you're in town, he may act as if he's in love. That's easy to do. Don't confuse a weekend of wine and roses with what this man may be like in day-to-day reality. A relationship takes more reality testing than that.

THE YOUNGSTER

I'm not talking about underage. I mean a youngster in terms of being younger and more naive than the man. Lots of men enjoy the ego stroking that comes from the feeling of being the older, more experienced man in the eyes of an admiring younger woman. It makes them feel important. What's more it makes them feel as if they haven't lost their touch. This scenario doesn't require a sixty-year-old man and a twenty-five-year-old woman. It could also be a thirty-five-year-old man and a twenty-seven-year-old woman. Or even a twenty-seven-year-old man and a twenty-one-year-old woman. The relationship still might have the same dynamics.

THE OLDER WOMAN

No bachelor's harem is complete without a so-called older woman. It's every young man's fantasy to have an older, more experienced lover, and today this isn't a problem. Women these days don't have to be ashamed of having younger men in their lives. Some actively pursue men many years their junior. Some of these women want a romantic tryst and others are looking for love. This makes it easy for the bachelor player to fill this position in his harem.

THE SINGLE MOM

Single moms are favorite targets of seasoned bachelor players. I know that comes as a surprise to many women. But it won't after I explain why. The single mother is busy—so busy that she doesn't have a lot of spare social time. Therefore, if she's dating, she is likely to want to squeeze as much into her free social time as possible. Enter King Solomon. He will use her limited time as a way to get sex without too much face time involved. He also knows that because she's busy, she can't place as many time demands on him as a single woman without kids.

Playing House

Some guys go a step further. Perhaps having a harem isn't enough. So they move in with a woman who has the qualities they would want in a wife, but they just don't marry her—instead, they play house. They live with her. They may even be committed. But they won't make the big *m* commitment. I find it an interesting phenomena in our society that people feel so comfortable mimicking marriage but not doing it when, in all practical realities, a couple playing house for any length of time is really acting basically as a married couple. In fact, in some states, such as Texas, where I live, so-called common law marriage is recognized as a marriage under some fairly easy-to-meet conditions. In other words, common sense tells us that a common law marriage *is* a marriage. Yet the fact that they haven't been required to actually make an official commitment allows many men in this situation to feel that they are free to break away when they desire. Once again, they avoid the responsibility and accountability that is natural and requisite to a relationship.

Women versus Women

Ironically, one of the most advantageous games for the bachelor player is a game he doesn't even play himself. It's the ongoing battle of women vs. women when it comes to getting a man. Let's face it, there are some really competitive women out there, and instead of putting their foot down with King Solomon their beloved, they take it out on each other.

What's interesting is that women who see women as the enemy are often looking at everything with a distorted vision. The real problem isn't the other woman, it's the man who is sitting back and encouraging it all to happen (directly or indirectly). Usually a typical woman vs. woman scenario has two women attempting to outdo each other at doing something for a man. They are both trying to give him sex, understanding, food, gifts, and even money. What's strange is that instead of seeing the clear truth—that the man needs to make a decision and stick with it—the two women fight it out. Sometimes literally. Jerry Springer wouldn't have a show if it weren't for men sitting back and pitting women against women. Once again, the real winner is the bachelor player. This ruthless competition between women allows him to take his pick of women. Additionally, this competition allows an unethical man to pit woman against woman to help him accomplish his desire to get what he wants from women without having to commit, be loyal, or be responsible.

Things to Think About

1. What are some ways a woman can ensure she is being treated with respect and dignity in a relationship?
2. Have you ever been in denial about an issue in a relationship that later became a big problem because it wasn't addressed?
3. Have you ever felt you were just one of many women a man you were seeing was involved with? What did you do and why?
4. Have you ever been part of a harem?

Journal Exercise

Have you ever felt that a man wanted to have all of the advantages of a relationship with you, but he didn't want to commit an equal amount of himself to the relationship? What was the turning point at which you realized you could no longer be giving more than you were receiving? What have you learned from that relationship that you can use/or are using in another relationship? Elaborate on these issues.

Inside the Mind of a
Bachelor, Part 1

Hello, ladies, my name is Rod Lambert and I'm a confirmed bachelor. I'll be guiding you through this book by telling you the story of myself, a man who will not go down the aisle until I am dragged kicking and screaming. But then there's my buddy, Eric Renfro. Eric's getting married soon and for the life of me I can't figure out why. Eric is a good-looking dude. Like me, he's six two with a strong and lean basketball player's body. I make decent money as an entry-level manager in a bank downtown, but it's Eric who really has it goin' on with money. He owns his own business designing, installing, and maintaining computer networks for businesses.

So anyway, Eric's getting married. I tried to talk him out of it. But he's determined. I think this girl, Cindy, has him really whipped. I mean, she's fine and all that, don't get me wrong. If he wasn't with her, I'd try to talk to her myself. And I have to admit, she's cool too. She doesn't trip on things like a lot of women. The girl's got a good job; she's a pharmacist. She also has a kid, and Eric loves the little girl and she loves him. But damn, that doesn't mean he has to go and get married and all!

I know Eric. He's a player like me. Or he used to be, because the man he's become isn't the same. He's been acting weird for about a year. I remember about a month before he met Cindy, he threw out his little black book. Just threw it away. Then he stopped club hoppin' with the fellas. He said he was tired of being a player and wanted a new life with one woman. Then a few weeks later he went to get his allergy prescription filled. Turns out Cindy had been working at that pharmacy for a year, but he just never went in there during the day except that one time, and there she was. He got his mack on. Like I said, the boy was one of the best players I know.

They've been together all the time since then. But it's not like that hot infatuation he's had that has come and gone with more women than I can remember; it's deeper than that. He and Cindy went through that stage, and, to my surprise, they settled into a real relationship.

So they're jumping the broom soon. But I begged him not to get married. I told him, "Why buy the cow when you can get the milk for free?" I mean, he's already got everything he would have if they were married. I know Cindy's taking care of him good in the sack because my boy Eric only likes freaks. They go out all the time, and when they aren't doing that they stay in and do corny family stuff with the little girl. So he's got a fine woman, he's playing daddy with the little girl and all, so why does he need to get married? He can have all that without really being locked in if he plays it the way I'm telling him. Right now he's getting all the benefits but doesn't have to pay full price.

You see, what I do when I get lonely for some real companionship is just start seeing the same girl a little more often. But I don't make a commitment, I just start going out with her on the weekends instead of just coming by late at night. Then, when I'm over the feeling that I need a girl-friend, which I usually realize when she starts getting too attached or placing demands on me, I back off again. No harm, no foul, right? The honey might be angry or hurt a little, but after I let her cool off and come back at her talking right, she always lets me right back in. See, that's the way to play it. But no, my boy Eric thinks he has to get married. All I can say is that I've been a good friend and tried to warn him.

Why End the Bachelor Party?

Imagine this scenario. You're at a big party being thrown just for you. The room is full of the opposite sex—and they're all smiles when you turn in their direction. So many delicious choices you don't know which way to turn. The food is great. The music is jumping. Everybody's having a good time. You feel good, really good. Wouldn't you want this feeling to last forever? Of course.

That is the way bachelors feel. Life is a big bachelor party, so why would they ever want it to end? Women, good friends, sports cars, and lots of disposable income. Could life get any better? The bachelor has lived all of his life to get to this point. He's free, he's over twenty-one, and he can spend the money in his pocket on high-priced toys. At this time in his life there are two things that preoccupy a man's thinking: pleasure and making money, which he perceives will bring him more pleasure. And for many bachelors, the word "pleasure" means S-E-X.

Of course, sex isn't all a bachelor wants or needs from women, but at a certain stage during his bachelorhood, that's what he thinks. To understand this thinking, women have to try to switch their point of view to that of a bachelor. For example, a young woman with a career and stable life is more likely than a man in the same situation to see a relationship as the final piece in an otherwise perfect picture. On the other hand, the young bachelor in the same situation sees having the career and stable life as props for the purpose of living out his fantasies of being King Solomon.

However, it's important to understand that it's not that bachelors don't want any sort of relationship. They just want a relationship that is completely convenient for them. If they want sex, they want to be able to dial it up. If they want to talk, they want to be able to dial it up. If they want to go on a wholesome date or a wild romp, they want to have that at their fingertips too. It's King Solomon syndrome.

The Bachelor Party

One of the best ways to observe this King Solomon syndrome is to go to a bachelor party. The following is my recollection of one of the typical bachelor parties I've attended.

Jerry and his best man, Otis, stood in the middle of the living room where the sofa and chairs had been moved out of the way for the show. Otis, well buzzed from beer, yelled, "Jerry, since this is your last night as a free man, we wanted to do something special for you. After this it will always be the same woman every night. So we wanted you to go out with a bang on your last night alive as a free man."

Then the music started booming out of speakers placed around the living room. It was one of those songs celebrating the almighty booty. Sir Mix A Lot's "Baby Got Back." Jerry was led to the center of the room where he sat down in a chair. Swarming around the room were about twenty half-drunk guys clapping and hooting in anticipation of what was to come. Then in came Cinnamon, the stripper. She was a high-priced star straight off the stage of one of the town's better known strip clubs. Cinnamon strutted in on clear three-inch-heels wearing a skin-tight neon green dress that barely made it to her thighs. Her fingernails were fluorescent orange and she wore matching lipstick. She danced around a little and then came out of the skirt. That left nothing but a thin black G-string, a tattoo on her ankle, and her three-inch heels. Before her act was over, she'd only be wearing the tattoo.

Then she went to work. She gyrated in Jerry's lap, running her tongue down the side of his face. Putting her head in his crotch. And finally mounting him chair style, placing his hands on her bare butt and dry humping him so hard the chair was rocking and squeaking. When she finished with him, he looked like he'd really had sex. Then she started going around the room doing various "tricks" with her body parts for tips. She bent over, putting her butt practically on one guy's nose. She slapped it and shook it for him. She went to another guy and threw her leg across his shoulder, putting her clean-shaved koochie right in his face. But that was nothing. I won't mention some of the other things she did. Who says you can't get anything for a dollar these days?

After that, she went back to Jerry, took him by the hand, and disappeared into a bedroom for what we were told was a private dance. The world will never know if that's all that happened. Her show didn't last a long time and I don't know how much money Cinnamon made that night, but she was literally dropping dollar bills as she left.

This bachelor party scenario perfectly illustrates the dilemma faced by bachelors when it comes to marriage and putting away the King Solomon syndrome. The dilemma is best illustrated by what the best man said in his announcement before the stripping act, by the actual stripper's act, and by the reaction of the guys in the room.

Let's look first at what Jerry's best man said when he announced the stripper—he said it was Jerry's last night of freedom; that is, the death of his role as King Solomon. Those don't sound like encouraging words of hopes for happiness after marriage. Especially when you consider they came from a man who was married himself. The message was clear. He was telling Jerry that he was about to cross a great divide into a land in which life could no longer be as much fun as he was used to it being. The underlying message being that bachelorhood is the only time when a man really lives and enjoys his life.

The next illustration of the King Solomon syndrome and the dilemma it causes bachelors can be found in the decadent dance. We all enjoyed watching Cinnamon work the room. This was several years ago, and I'd be lying if I said I wasn't clapping, hooting and hollering, and tipping Cinnamon for her "tricks" myself. I was enjoying the entertainment. I was a different man then. But that doesn't change the fact that a stripper embodies another thing that bachelors love. The stripper is the fantasy paramour without a commitment. The only commitment a man has with a stripper is money. That makes him feel comfortable because she can't make any demands of him, and it gives him a degree of control over the situation. For that money, she is willing to play whatever role he wants. If he wants wild erotic dancing, she'll do that. If he wants a slow sensual dance, she can do that. If he wants her to sit and talk and make him feel important, she will do that. It's an illusion and an odd quid pro quo.

The last illustration of our King Solomon syndrome was the crowd's raucous approval of what was going on. Probably one of the most influential factors in the behavior of bachelors is how we lead each other by example. From the looks of it, these guys and I were all having a really good time. This is a story that would be told in offices, locker rooms, and bars all over the country when these guys went home after the wedding weekend. The stories we took back to our male friends about this night would serve to reinforce the same behavior in them and other men.

The bachelor party was wild. But the next afternoon we all assembled at the church for the wedding. There we stood at the front of the church in our tuxedos. Most of us were single and committed to bachelorhood. Even as the reverend spoke, I wonder how many of the guys were still thinking about Cinnamon.

Looking back on it now, I can see the pattern behind our actions. Bachelorhood moves in stages, and many of us were in what I call the exploration stage of bachelorhood. That's a time when the last thing a man wants to do is to be married; and therefore, he shouldn't be.

The Three Stages of Bachelorhood

Bachelorhood moves in three distinct stages:

Discovery stage ➤ **Exploration stage** ➤ **Conversion stage**

DISCOVERY STAGE

The discovery stage is when a man realizes he's an official bachelor. For some men this starts early, in their late teens upon graduating high school, particularly if they skip college and go directly into the workforce or the military. But for many men, the discovery stage of bachelorhood doesn't really kick into full gear until they graduate from college.

At this point in the young bachelor's life, he's just beginning to realize that he has absolute and total freedom to do anything he wants. He has his own income and likely has no dependents. This creates the disposable income that will pay for, among other indulgences, a sports car. During this stage women are seen as part of the young bachelor's recreation. Women are part of the fun props he will use to make himself happy. However, he is not yet a skilled player and will make some mistakes as he perfects his Don Juan act and enters the exploration stage.

EXPLORATION STAGE

In the exploration stage, the young bachelor has learned the lessons of being a player. He's picked up cues from other players and he's had his own practical experiences to draw from. Now he's ready to capitalize on what he's learned. In the discovery stage, he didn't know his worth on the romantic market. But during the exploration phase, he's keenly aware of his worth as a bachelor. He understands that being an eligible bachelor gives him power with women. Particularly if he's a handsome professional man with a high income or a moderate but stable income. He maximizes his leverage by having several women, assembling his harem. He may even have a girlfriend. But he won't commit to anything long term. She's more of a trophy or status symbol.

CONVERSION STAGE

The conversion stage is the shortest of the stages. In fact, it's really not as much a stage as it is a moment of reckoning. This is the time when something triggers a bachelor's interest in steady and committed relationships and the desire to find a wife. For some men, it's a point they come to after realizing there's got to be more to life than just living life as a swinging bachelor. For others, it may be the possibility of losing a relationship with a woman they have grown to love. Or it could be a need to fill a void that can be completed only by the intimate union of a man and woman. Whatever the cause, when this stage comes, it is the launching pad for the next phase of life for a man.

NOTE ABOUT THE STAGES OF BACHELORHOOD

Bachelors of any age can be in any of the various stages of bachelorhood. For example, a middle-aged man who goes through a divorce will typically start his love life over with new discovery and exploration stages, before proceeding to the conversion stage and entering into another long-term relationship or marriage.

Reasons Some Bachelors Never Seem to Change

However, some men don't transition so smoothly from bachelorhood. Instead, they get stuck in the exploration stage. The following are reasons some men have difficulty transitioning out of bachelorhood.

SOME BACHELORS DON'T WANT TO GROW UP

Some guys can't seem to make the transition from bachelor to marriage, or even a committed relationship. I recall the film *Forces of Nature* with Ben Affleck playing a reluctant bachelor who was about to grow up and become a groom. The only problem was that he wasn't really doing something he seemed to want to do. This film really illustrated well the case of reluctant grooms. But of course in typical Hollywood fashion, the story ends with Affleck's character being magically transformed at the end and being ready to get married. I'm not saying that that can't and doesn't happen. But it's not always reality. In reality, people get married everyday who shouldn't be. In Hollywood, the ending fixes everything and people live happily ever after. But in reality, bachelors sometimes go through with weddings they've changed their minds about simply because the invitations are printed and they don't want to be embarrassed.

SOME MEN SEE WOMEN AS OBJECTS OR TROPHIES

Bachelors who see women only as sexual objects or trophies objectify women. They don't see women as potential life partners. They see them only as useful for fulfilling some sort of ego-boosting purpose in their self-absorbed world.

SOME MEN ARE LOOKING
FOR MOTHERS

Another type of bachelor can't seem to transition out of the bachelor world because he's the infamous mama's boy. This is the man who isn't looking for a wife; he's looking for a mother, someone to take responsibility for him as well as do all of his washing, cooking, and cleaning.

SOME MEN SEE SEX AS A SPORT

This is a mentality some men don't get beyond regardless of age: the caveman feeling that when he sees a woman he likes, he has to conquer her—meaning he has to get her into bed. For this man, a woman is a symbol of his sexual prowess and his masculinity. He feels that if he can get a particular woman into bed, he has in some sense proven his ability as a man.

SOME MEN WANT TO HANG OUT
WITH THE BOYS FOREVER

There are guys that would rather hang out with the boys than be in a relationship that places demands on their time and energy. This doesn't make them bad people, but it's a clear choice of priorities. I remember a time when I was single that I felt this way, and it was perfectly okay because I remained unattached. If he'd rather go hang out or run the streets with his boys, that's what he should do (within responsible bounds, of course). But he can't have a relationship during his development stage. Please note: This doesn't mean that a man should *ever* have to choose between his friends or having a girlfriend or wife. Unfortunately, this is the way men sometimes feel, even beyond the developmental stage, and some women contribute to that feeling.

SOME MEN HAVE NO VISION FOR LIFE, OR HAVE A SELFISH VISION

Another guy who isn't ready for marriage is the guy who has no vision for his life. Anyone who is married can tell you that marriage is no place for a person who isn't grounded enough to at least have an idea of what he or she wants to do with their life.

On the other hand, there's the guy who has a vision for what he wants to do with his life, but it's all about him. He's even more dangerous to get involved with because he is not about *we*, he's about me.

A FINAL NOTE

The bachelor mind-set is not about age! Please don't make the common mistake of thinking that the bachelor mind-set occurs only in the twenties and early thirties, because that's not the case. Bachelors come in all ages. And though most of this book is written about the young-and-restless variety, there are guys who are middle-aged and even older who still have the same characteristics as the younger bachelors. It's not about age, it's about personal maturity and growth.

Also, I don't mean to imply that simply because a man isn't married, he's stuck in bachelorhood. For more on that topic, refer to Chapter 4, "Groom-o-Phobia."

Cultural Cues That Tell Men Not to End the Bachelor Party

Men get some very clear and distinct messages about the power and privilege of bachelorhood from all aspects of society, including the very women who complain about bachelors being uncommitted to the idea of relationships and marriage. Here are some of the main social cues bachelors receive.

IT'S TIME TO SOW YOUR WILD OATS

Nobody has to tell a young man with hot hormones throbbing through his veins to sow his wild oats. He's going to do it anyway. Yet we indirectly and directly tell young men to do this. I can recall women I dated saying things such as "I know you have lots of girlfriends." Or "I know you have others, but I'd have to be number one." The message to me was "Bachelorhood is my party, and I can have as many women as I want."

Indirectly, men are told to sow their wild oats through

more subtle cues. For example, when older men reminisce and tell young bachelors about how they played the women back in their day. Or married men chiding bachelors to "enjoy the fun while it lasts." Or women who make sexually suggestive remarks about a man being a bachelor while giving a sneaky smile as if to silently signal that she knows he's out there sowing his wild oats and it's commendable.

Another indirect signal bachelors receive is found in the term "settling down." When I was single, people always asked me, "When are you going to settle down and get married?" Words mean a lot. And to ask a man when he's going to settle down implies that as a single man he isn't supposed to feel settled. Furthermore, the implication is that he will have to one day "settle down" and become serious, which feeds into the very idea that commitment and marriage isn't a step up but rather a loss of freedom.

YOU'RE IN HIGH DEMAND

Every time a statistic about men being in short supply runs on the news, one can just feel the shock wave of panic in women. As a result, some women start acting out of fear. I have had discussions with women who know a man has another woman and are okay with that. These women aren't in a casual dating situation but an actual relationship. They consider themselves lucky to be in a relationship with a man even if he's involved with other women as well. You do the math. I say one plus two equals three, and in a relationship three's a crowd.

THE POWERFUL MYSTIQUE SURROUNDING ELIGIBLE MEN

Bachelor mania seems to grip our country in various ways. One way is the furor over the media's annual bachelor lists. For example, *Ebony* magazine and *People* magazine feature eligible bachelors each year, and women all over the country swoon. Women who desire to be married see these handsome men with high-caliber careers and buy the magazines to fuel their hopes of finding a Mr. Right. Some of them even write in to try to contact some of the men they see. This is an example of how highly desirable bachelors achieve power from the mystique surrounding eligible bachelors. Since they have the ability to be, or at least have the appearance of being, Prince Charming, they acquire a certain degree of power. Furthermore, for some men, this mystique and allure of being single and available is actually profitable. Some actors and entertainers directly benefit from the fact that they are single. Their female fans want them that way because they feel that, at least vicariously, they have that man in their lives. If they were married, they'd lose some of their allure and thus a part of their popularity. There's definitely a feeling of power associated with being an eligible bachelor.

Things to Think About

1. Do you think single men who are in high demand have their way with women too easily?
2. How should a woman respond when a highly desirable man is interested in her?
3. What are women doing that encourages highly desirable men to feel unaccountable?

Journal Exercise

Do you feel men have an advantage in the singles market? If you do, how does this affect the way you interact with men who are interested in you? Reflect on times when you have felt an eligible bachelor with whom you were involved was attempting to use his high demand to his advantage. How did you deal with the situation? Write about how you can maintain your dignity while dating or seeking a desirable mate.

Inside the Mind of a Bachelor, Part 2

Eric got married this weekend. I was one of the best men. I stood there and watched him come down the aisle with that stupid complacent smile on his face. Like I said, the man has gone insane. He's got it all and now he's got to go and ruin it by getting married. Mark my words, his black Corvette will be the first thing to go, probably replaced by a minivan. Then she'll make him get rid of the town house so she can strap him down somewhere in the suburbs with a fat mortgage waking him up every morning. Next comes the first kid, then the second, and poof! The next time I see him he'll be balding and thirty pounds overweight!

As for me, no thanks. I'm having too much fun right now. It's all about me, baby! Take the wedding, for example. I got numbers from two babes at the wedding. One hotty, Nancy, was one of the bridesmaids. I was talking to her the night of the rehearsal dinner and got the digits. I had to be smooth with her because she knew she had it goin' on. She was so tight that I was even a little nervous when I asked for her number. First, she did that "You give me yours and I'll call you" stuff. But I kept talking to her all night and she finally gave up the number.

The other one I got the digits from was Yvette, this tight babe who was signing people in to the guest book the afternoon of the wedding. I saw her the night of the rehearsal dinner while I was rapping to Nancy. I have to admit, I almost went for her, but instead she came in a close second place. But at the reception, I had a chance to talk with her while Nancy was preoccupied doing things with the bride. Within minutes I knew Yvette was down for some action. She was giving me the "can you handle this woman?" look and speaking all sultry and stuff. I got her digits and that was that. I'll let you know how it all turns out. But I can tell you right now, I'll be hittin' that before the week's over. It's Nancy, the bridesmaid, who'll be a challenge. Like I said, she knows she's got it going on. Besides, she's one of those babes who's looking for a relationship, I can tell. But I know she's got needs like any other woman. I'll just have to figure out which buttons to push.

3

Why So Many "Mr. Rights" Aren't Interested in Marriage

Here's an issue that starkly illustrates the differences between the sexes. So many eligible women seem to be ready, willing, and able to step to the altar with the right man, but it seems as if bachelors are averse to the idea of marriage. Single women see it as a beginning; bachelors see it as an end. Just what is it that makes Mr. Right so often turn into Mr. Not Right Now?

Who Is Your Mr. Right?

Before we can discuss why the Mr. Rights out there aren't stepping up to the altar, it's important for you to define exactly who Mr. Right is to you. Defining your Mr. Right is a critical step in your understanding of him and therefore his perspective on marriage and relationships. On the following list, pretend you have a Man Building Machine that you can program to generate any man you imagine. Attempt to be as precise as possible in your definition of your own Mr. Right.

Also, to add a touch of reality to your list, you're limited to ten points per category. In other words, you must prioritize what is most important to you by giving it a number between zero and ten, zero being of no importance and ten being the most important. Remember, the total for each category can't exceed ten. That is, to be a perfect ten on one choice within a category means your Mr. Right will have to score zeroes on all of the other choices within that category. However, you may split your ten points between as many choices within a category as you desire. For example, you could have a combination of two points on one choice, zero points on a choice, five points on another choice, and three points on yet another choice, all totaling ten points for that category. Now, go for it; build your Mr. Right.

Basic Physical Characteristics

Height _____

Age _____

Weight _____

Hair color _____

Skin shade _____

Physical appearance _____

Muscular build _____

Medium build _____

Slim build _____

Handsome _____

Pretty boy _____

Rugged _____

Average looks _____

Personality Traits

Humor and wit _____

Strong, silent type _____

Take-charge type _____

Studious/scholarly _____

Expressive _____

Athletic _____

Education

Not important _____

At least GED/High school _____

College degree _____

Graduate degree _____

Ph.D./M.D./J.D./Professional designation
(CPA, AIA, etc.) _____

Family History

Nuclear family with mother/father in
home _____

No divorced/estranged parents _____

Raised with influence of strong
father/mother _____

Middle-class background _____

Wealthy background _____

Working-class background _____

Has overcome an economically disadvantaged background _____

Relationship History

Never been married _____

Divorced _____

Single and has not had any serious relationships _____

Single and has had at least one serious relationship _____

Single and has had several serious relationships _____

Income

High _____

Comfortable _____

Stability is more important than amount _____

Profession

Professional _____

Entrepreneur _____

Creative (actor, artist, writer) _____

Law enforcement/Emergency services _____

Blue collar/Skilled laborer/Craftsman _____

Educator _____

Other _____

Not important _____

His Most Valued Personal Goals

Wealth and luxury _____

Having a family _____

Travel _____

Peaceful life _____

His Goals for a Family

Wants a child ⸺⸺

Wants two or three children ⸺⸺

Wants a large family ⸺⸺

Doesn't want children ⸺⸺

Open to adoption ⸺⸺

Open to artificial methods ⸺⸺

Now that you've completed the list, imagine the man of your dreams. How did your fantasy man rate against your man from the list? One thing should be absolutely clear from your list: You're going to have to make some compromises. I didn't say you had to settle for less than you feel you deserve, but you will have to compromise because no man is going to be perfect, even if he's a great catch.

Settling versus Compromising

Before moving on, I want to emphasize the difference between settling and compromising. Here's the rule. Never settle for less than you deserve, but always be willing to compromise. The difference is a fine line, but it makes all the difference in the world in your success with picking the right bachelor with whom to pursue a relationship and marriage.

Settling is a bad thing because settling is to accept defeat. When you settle for a relationship with a man you don't really love, you're doomed for unhappiness. Think about how bad you feel when you have to settle on your second choice for an apartment, car, or job. To imagine what that's like in terms of settling in a relationship, multiply that unhappiness by one thousand because when you settle in a relationship, you're dealing with a human being, which is much more difficult than redecorating the second choice apartment or trading in your car for a better model.

In contrast, to accept that compromise is necessary is just plain reality. Compromising is what you did when you designed your Mr. Right and had to restrict yourself to ten points per category. Utilizing such an exercise reinforces that we can't have it all in one person, but we can find someone who has the most important traits we desire. We simply have to accept the rest of that person with the deal.

Reasons Some Mr. Right Types Give for Putting Marriage Off

Now that you've defined your Mr. Right and have his image firmly in mind, we can discuss him in more detail. As a generic concept of Mr. Right, I'll define him as a reasonably attractive, economically viable single man. I obtained the following reasons for putting marriage off from men possessing those characteristics.

SO MANY WOMEN, SO LITTLE TIME

> *I know women don't meet a lot of guys who can speak well, hold the door open for them, and all that stuff. That's how I get 'em. Most of these guys have such weak game that when a brother like me comes along with a good job, his own business, and treating a woman well too. . . . I can have whatever I want from a woman.*
> —*Jordan, age 27, dentist*

To be quite frank about it, highly desirable Mr. Right types play the odds in their favor. They know women have choices of the men they pursue relationships with, but they also realize that there aren't many men like them to choose from.

The first thing a guy who's got a good job, education, and social graces realizes is that he has virtually unlimited access to women. He doesn't come to this realization by researching the U.S. Census statistics to see that there are more women than men. Rather, he learns of his value through the behavior of women. An eligible bachelor receives cues from women that tell him he's a hot commodity. Sometimes bachelors don't even have to read cues; they get a direct appraisal of their value. For example, a female friend of mine once said to me, "William, a man like you could have two or three women and they all wouldn't care about the other woman if you played it right." She went on to explain that it was because I was a so-called good catch and that some women would rather have a part of a good man than all of a bad one.

Most men aren't saints. When they hear these appraisals of their value to women as priceless treasures, they're inevitably going to exploit the odds. I won't even pretend to say that I didn't. Even the so-called good men are susceptible to doing it because saying no to the myriad opportunities they get takes a self-discipline and restraint that few men have.

WOMEN COMPETING WITH WOMEN

I was at a home watching television one night when I got a call from my girlfriend's roommate. My girlfriend had gone home for the weekend and her roommate went into her phone book, got my number, and called me. She was talking like she wanted me to come over and jump her bones.

—William, age 22, college student

One of the reasons some Mr. Rights resist getting married is the way some women willingly compete with other women for their attention. They benefit from this competition because it continuously brings new women to them. It sounds diabolical, but it isn't as sinister as it sounds be-

cause it's not always the man who pits woman versus
woman. Many women seem to do it automatically. The big
winner is the bachelor; he benefits from each woman trying to perform better than the next woman because she's
motivated by the fear that if she doesn't keep him happy,
another woman will step in to take her place.

This subject is also covered in Chapter 1, "Why Buy
the Cow When You Can Get the Milk for Free?"

A BETTER WOMAN MAY BE JUST AROUND THE CORNER

> *Since I'm a pilot, I'm always traveling and I meet some
> incredibly interesting and beautiful women all over the
> country all the time. That makes it hard for me to settle
> down because I know as soon as I fly out again, I'm
> going to meet one who blows away the one I just met.*
> —*Claude, age 37, pilot*

Some Mr. Rights aren't interested in marriage because
they live in the fear that a better woman is just about to surface in their lives and if they commit, they'll miss out. This
is because of the previously explained bachelor party mentality. At a party, you never know who's going to walk
through the door next. That's part of the excitement. Therefore, until a guy gets beyond that mentality, he's always going to neglect to see what's right in front of him because he's
so busy watching the door for the next woman to walk in.

HE'S AFRAID MARRIAGE WILL
RUIN A GOOD RELATIONSHIP

*Thinking about marriage sort of scares me because it
seems like people stop having a good time. After a while
you wonder why they are even together.*
                    —Eugene, age 29, Army lieutenant

Some guys have no experience of having good relationships. Or they only recall having good relationships when
things were kept at a safe level—that is, when they weren't
too serious. Therefore, they remain in a state of suspension
in their relationships. They fear that if they commit, it will
be something that they, or both of them as a couple, won't be
able to handle. They know that a marriage would bring real
demands on their time and energy that they aren't sure they
will be able to meet so they avoid moving to that next level.

CAREER DEMANDS

*Marriage? No, thanks. I have a fast-paced career and it
takes all of my time and energy. My girlfriends don't
understand that so I don't feel a wife would.*
                    —Tom, age 38, professional speaker

Whenever I write or speak to a female audience on the
subject of relationships or marriage, I always take time to

emphasize how important a man's career is to his feeling of success and overall self-esteem. It may not always preclude his getting married, but it certainly does occupy a central role in his life. Therefore, the timing involved when a man decides to get married is crucial. Usually a man doesn't want to get married until he feels he is at least on the path toward achieving his career goals.

Also, for many men, their fantasy of success in life ideally wouldn't include getting married until after they'd had the opportunity to live at the highest level of bachelorhood. That means having a high income, an expensive car, and a luxurious bachelor pad, and dating desirable women. If they had their way, many men would choose to get married only after having tired of that sort of lifestyle.

What About Men Who Just Don't Get Married?

My wife and I were both speaking in Pennsylvania at a conference, and while there we made a trip to Amish country. One of the places we visited was the home of President James Buchanan, known as the bachelor president. The tour guide explained to us that since he was a bachelor, he had to have his niece move in to be the woman of the house. In those days, a house could not be a home without a woman on the premises to be "the lady of the house." His niece dutifully served in that role until her marriage, at which time his maid was promoted to the position.

Though that sounds like old-fashioned thinking, it's

alive and well today. Often men, particularly those who are successful, are stereotyped as selfish, promiscuous, unstable, strange, or even gay if they aren't married or in a relationship. But some men don't desire to be married. Marriage isn't for everyone, and some men simply won't fool themselves into believing they want to be married. We shouldn't feel it's necessary to gossip about them or attempt to psychoanalyze them for making this decision. In fact, if more people were honest with themselves about their feelings regarding marriage, I'll bet the divorce rate wouldn't be quite as high because some of those people wouldn't have ever married in the first place. Yet many people do succumb to the social pressures to get married; they feel it's easier to be married than to continue to answer questions about why they aren't married or have friends feel it's necessary to play matchmaker for them.

For men in this situation, this pressure can be summarized in three myths:

1. If he's not married by a certain point, he must be gay.
2. If he's not married, there must be something wrong with him or something strange about him.
3. If he's not married, he must be lazy or irresponsible.

Sure, like all assumptions, these could be true in some cases, but they are definitely not true in all cases. Remain open-minded and consider the possibility that a man may purposely choose a more solitary life.

Things to Think About

1. After creating your Mr. Right in this chapter, how realistic do you think your perception of Mr. Right is?
2. What do you feel are bachelors' valid concerns and fears about marriage?
3. What do you feel are bachelors' unsubstantiated or contrived concerns and fears about marriage?
4. Do you feel marriage is for everyone? Why or why not?

Journal Exercise

It's not just men who have concerns and fears about marriage; women do too. What are some of the concerns or fears you have about marriage? What do you feel is the basis of those fears? For example, it may be prior experience or the advice of friends and relatives. Write about how you plan to engage those issues constructively.

Inside the Mind of a Bachelor, Part 3

You remember Yvette, the honey from the wedding who was signing people in to the guest book? Mission accomplished. Yep, last night, I hit that. I called her up, we talked for a while, and I started making comments about her needing a massage, you know, basic lines to feel her out. She came right back at me and we passed up the formalities and cut to the chase. I went over and gave her a full-body treatment, if you know what I mean. It was good and I'll be back for more, especially since she wasn't all clinging to me when I told her I had to leave.

I haven't talked to the other babe, Nancy, yet. I'm waiting to see if she'll call me first. But if I'm right about her type, I know she won't call me first because she probably knows I'm not looking for a relationship and all that stuff. When chicks like her know you're not serious, they usually don't call. That's why I had to sweat her even to get her number.

I don't know; part of me wants to call her and part of me doesn't. I mean, she's tight and all that. But I know I'm going to have to come correct with her. I'm going to have to talk with her on the phone, then go out with her and all that. Eventually, if she feels safe with me, she'll give it up. But she'll also feel like we're moving toward a relationship and I'll have to deal with her trippin' when she realizes I'm not going there. I've been down that road before. But why do all that when I can just get out the black book and play dial-a-babe?

Yet something still makes me want to call her. Eric was right, in a sense; playing the field is getting old. I'm not going to lie. Some Friday afternoons after a hard week, I'd love to go home to a babe like Nancy and just chill. She was really cool. Sort of like Eric's girl, Cindy. If I was going to chill with somebody, it would definitely be with a babe like her.

But see, I just can't settle down right now. I mean, there

are just too many other women out there for me to meet. Just look at my office building. There are enough babes there that it would take me a year to meet all of them. It would be my luck that I'd just start all that relationship stuff with Nancy, and then I'd meet some hotty in my office building. Then there are the honeys at the gym, the babes at church, the chicks at the mall and of course the clubs. The possibilities for a brother like me are endless. Why mess up like my boy Eric?

Besides, I'm up for the fast-track management training program this year. If I get into that program, and I plan to, I'll have training sessions three or four nights a week for a year. The last thing I need is some babe calling me up asking me where I am all the time. It's just not a good time for me to deal with a girl like Nancy.

4

Groom-o-Phobia

There I was, standing ready at the Hilton Waterfront in New Orleans. I was dressed in a tuxedo. I was one of the groomsmen in my friend Dobbin's wedding. Always a groomsman and never a groom. And I liked it that way.

After the traditional wedding ceremony, we all assembled in the ballroom for the reception. We smiled for some photos, toasted the newlyweds with champagne, and cheered as they cut the cake. It was going well until the tossing of the garter was announced. All the single guys knew what that meant. As the folklore goes, the man to catch the garter will be the next to marry. None of us wanted to be the one.

Suddenly a curious phenomenon occurred. It was as

if an alien ship were hovering above the Hilton's ballroom. A roomful of eligible bachelors suddenly froze into stiff poses—our arms became rigid, our faces took on blank stares, and we couldn't move. Not one of us headed toward the front of the ballroom. Another call came for the single men to approach the dance floor. Realizing the threat was imminent, we took action and all started slowly creeping backward. A third call. Then I felt someone's arm hook mine and pull me through the crowd to the front. About twenty stone-faced men had been herded the same way and stood there awkwardly. We were silent, shifting our weight from foot to foot, waiting for it to be over.

Dobbin turned his back toward us and flung the garter over his head. It swirled in the air. We scattered. I've never seen so many men in a room have a sudden need to check their watches. One brother folded his arms and dropped his head. Others looked away as if distracted. I stuck my hands in my pockets and pursed my lips, "Oh, God, please don't let it land near me," I thought.

—*William July,* Brothers, Lust and Love

Why Grooms Get Groom-o-Phobia, or Cold Feet

All bachelors are afraid of marriage. They all have groom-o-phobia, or cold feet, a temporary condition that strikes fear of marriage into their hearts. I don't care if a guy is head over heels in love and can picture himself with a woman for the rest of his life living happily ever after, he's still afraid of being a groom. If he says it doesn't scare him, then he's lying to impress you.

What's ironic is that men are not totally terrified of the idea of being married. Men want to be married, have kids, and live happily ever after just like women do. But they have to get past their fears of being a groom first. The act of being a groom is a unique rite of passage for men from bachelorhood, defined as carefree living, across a bridge into the married world of responsibility, accountability, and coexistence. It can be daunting.

Here's a sample of what a man is juggling mentally as the date approaches:

As a single man, the little black book is in full swing. Most single guys have a harem. They might not call it that, but that's essentially what it is. They have a group of women they actively date who are readily available to them. Some of those women may be aware of that and not care (because they're doing the same thing), and some of them may think there's some sort of relationship going on. One reason bachelors build harems is so they can avoid having to deal with issues that crop up in relationships. If he feels a woman is acting up or trippin'—that is, being too much trouble for him—he rotates her out of the lineup the way the manager of a baseball team pulls out a pitcher and puts in one he's had warming up in the bullpen. As you can see, a harem isn't just about sex, it's about having it all the bachelor's way. As a married man, he loses that privilege. Married men have to face their problems and issues with their wives because they live and sleep with them exclusively. This is something the bachelor has been avoiding.

Then, of course, there's the issue of monogamy. Settling down can be an overwhelming idea for a man who has spent the past few years bouncing from woman to woman at will. Again, if a man tells you this doesn't scare him, he's either from another planet or he's lying to impress you. Monogamy scares *all* men. The purely biological part of a man doesn't want to settle down. Getting married is a higher function of thinking and behavior in which a man has to overcome the simply animalistic tendencies he is prone to by virtue of biology. In other words, to really not be absolutely terrified of monogamy, he's got to be at a point in his mental and spiritual development at which he can overcome purely biological urges. Not all men are ready for monogamy. In fact, I daresay some will never be. Marriage takes a willingness and a commitment to the act of monogamy. It doesn't just happen. If you look at the bachelor's life, it's not about monogamy, it's about the exact opposite, characterized by the sowing of his wild oats and getting it out of his system. The problem is that neither of these ideas actually works. In fact, I tell younger guys to try to have some restraint as bachelors because the more women they date, the harder it will be later actually to commit to one woman. And though they don't know it when they're cruising around being bachelors, there will come a time when they will want to be with one woman.

That's when all of their past will come back either to make monogamy easier or to haunt them.

Things previously unimportant suddenly become magnified for a bachelor when he gets married. The first example that comes to mind is something very simple: eating. For a bachelor, it's a simple process. You're driving down the street and you choose from the fast food offerings that jump out at you. Or you scoop up a to-go order from a restaurant. Simple. Done. Go home and reach over the empty pizza cartons in the refrigerator and grab some orange juice, pour a glass, and sit down with your hot wings and OJ as you glue your mind to ESPN. But that changes for a married man, and bachelors are aware of this—though I don't think they realize the full extent of this change.

I clearly remember that one of the shocks I had after being married was the whole idea of grocery shopping. As a single man, I used to pick up a few things from the store now and then; generally I ate out. Cooking was something my kitchen experienced only on occasion. But after getting married and having a wife and a stepdaughter, I wasn't just casually dropping in the store once in a while to pick up a loaf of bread, grapes, and orange juice. Suddenly I was *shopping*. It was really unfamiliar territory for me. My only experience grocery shopping was memories of hanging on the basket as my mother pushed it down the aisle. Now my wife was handing me lists with little detailed things on them that I didn't even know were in the store. Then . . . cha-ching, the register was ringing up amounts of money that I didn't even know could be spent on groceries. It was a quick lesson in economies of scale. I had gone from my bachelor grocery shopping, which required only a hand basket, a few minutes, and a few dollars, to full-scale shopping with a basket so full I could hardly steer it and a whopping bill.

Another previously inane detail to bachelors that becomes life sized when they are married is furniture. Furniture is a simple issue of economics in a bachelor pad. If a guy is fresh out of school and just getting established, he keeps it simple. A stereo system. An entertainment system to hold his television, videos, and CDs. A sofa and a table to prop his feet on. The bedroom consists of a mattress on the floor. The kitchen is a refrigerator and a stove that has never done more than heat pizza, boil wieners, or scramble eggs.

When he gets a little more money, he moves to phase two, and things get a little more stylish. He'll buy a better stereo, a bigger television, and, oh yes, a bedroom set, black lacquer, of course. He may even stop by a department store and pick up a few decorations for the house. He'll buy some pots and pans on the false promise to himself that he's going to start cooking more.

In phase three, instead of a bigger television and a better stereo, he'll go all out with the customized home entertainment center with Dolby stereo and Surround Sound. He usually conceives of his decor by looking in magazines or taking one of his girlfriends with him to do the shopping and decorating. This bachelor will have a place that has all the details and right touches because he can afford it.

But when they get married, most bachelors aren't at phase three, they're in either phase one or two with furniture. So here is yet another situation in which they will suffer from massive sticker shock: going furniture shopping. Part of getting married is the process of starting a nest. Starting a nest includes getting new furniture. You can imagine how shocked the bachelor is when he finds out how much a good sofa with a hideaway bed costs. (His mom gave him the sofa he currently has.) Just imagine the horror on his face when his fiancée is enamored with the "great price" on a rosewood dining room table.

Fear of the Unknown

Getting married is moving from a known routine to mysterious and uncharted seas. In his mind, the bachelor knows that marriage ultimately will lead to things such as buying a home and having children, and that having all of these things will depend on his producing income to sustain his family. The bachelor who gives the requisite serious thought to the role of husband and father will no doubt find it a challenge. If he takes his marital vows seriously, he sees that he is signing up for a journey in life that will call for the very best in him. Such a realization always prompts a person into a self-assessment, which can be a time of high anxiety because of self-doubt.

Keeping His Feet Warm

Assuming a man is ready, willing, and able to get married, you can take some reasonable measures to prevent cold feet. Here are some ways you can prevent—or significantly lessen—premarital jitters.

1. Don't get engaged and set the wedding for a date ten years later.

Getting engaged and putting the wedding off for too long is a sure way to invite a bachelor to get cold feet. Set your wedding date within a reasonable amount of time to make arrangements and do it! Of course, I don't mean to imply that you should just rush to the altar on an impulse. That's a terrible idea. Getting married sooner rather than later is based on the assumption that you're dealing with a ready, willing, and able groom.

If you must have a huge wedding a year or more from the date of the engagement, keep his feet warm by not allowing the details to suffocate him (or you). Keep the relationship hot and spicy, and don't become so focused on the wedding that the two of you stop being what brought you together in the first place.

2. Have a small wedding and just get it over with.

As Nike ads say, "Just do it!" If you intend to get married, why not have a small ceremony with a reasonable budget for family and close friends, and go ahead and get married? Or an even smaller wedding is an idea. For example, my wife and I had a ceremony in which we each had a couple of best friends present, as well as the minister, our parents, and a few immediate relatives. There were less than twenty people in the small chapel. Another option is to have a small ceremony of your choosing, a small reception or party afterward, and a honeymoon if your budget allows. If not, you can do that later.

**3. Get married at the courthouse
and have a ceremony later.**
I think wedding ceremonies are important because they serve a spiritual function by allowing two people to bond with the blessings of their loved ones. However, I also think getting married at the courthouse is just fine as an option when a ceremony, large or small, is inconvenient or not financially viable.

Things That Women Do to Give Bachelors Groom-o-Phobia, or Cold Feet

SHE MAKES ASSUMPTIONS ABOUT MARRIAGE PLANS
Some women tell men up front what they're looking for in a relationship; for instance, some will tell a guy they're looking for a man with whom they can have a long-term re-

lationship leading to marriage. That's cool. That's just putting your cards on the table. However, another type of woman out there doesn't simply put her cards on the table; this woman just flat out assumes that a man she's dating is going to marry her. Or, in worse cases, she thinks she's going to get him to start thinking about marriage from day one through dropping subtle and not-so-subtle hints.

I remember dating a very nice woman in whom I was interested. However, I couldn't take her constant hints about marriage. Actually, her willingness to think about marriage was frightening to me because we'd only been out a couple of times when she started dropping little hints about us as a married couple. On one date, we were coming back from a movie one Sunday afternoon and passing a subdivision being constructed. She asked me to drive through. Thinking nothing of it, I whisked in and we admired the fine homes under construction. That's when her hints about marriage went from hints to statements of fact, such as "We should get one like that." Followed by "I think I'll only work part time after our first child." By this time, we were on about our fourth date, and yes, there was chemistry. But she was moving far too fast for me in the assumptions about marriage, and it scared me off.

SHE MAKES A DATE FEEL LIKE A POTENTIAL HUSBAND INSTEAD OF A DATE

Just as there are trophy wives, there are trophy husbands. Trophy husbands are men with good jobs, good looks, and great personalities. Like beautiful women, these men often find themselves being courted for their attributes first and for who they are as people second. In other words, these men become accustomed to women wanting to date them because they're a good catch. Now, this is certainly a compliment. However, just because a guy is a good catch doesn't mean a relationship will automatically have that intangible chemistry necessary to make it bond passionately and faithfully.

Women who date men first as potential husbands and secondarily for who they are as people evaluate everything in terms of how it would play out in a marriage. In essence, they skip getting to know a bachelor for who he is as a person. One good catch put it this way: "I used to have a girlfriend who thought of everything we did in terms of marriage. She was always talking about what a good husband I'd make. It would have been a compliment except she was more concerned about that than she was about our relationship. She was so far down the road with all that husband stuff that she didn't see that her image of me as a husband was all we had in common."

SHE INTRODUCES DETAILS
OF HER LIFE TOO EARLY

As an author friend of mine, J. S. McCord, always says, "All of God's children have issues." But for heaven's sake, don't unload a dump truck full of issues on a man right away. Yes, everyone has issues and problems, but the first or second date isn't always the time to discuss them—unless, of course, they could somehow impact the health or safety of the other person. This isn't to say you should play a role and pretend to be too good to be true. It just means that tact is necessary, along with good timing.

For example, I was getting to know a really nice-looking girl who'd caught my eye at a shopping mall. During our first conversation on the phone, the subject of the last people we dated came up. I told her a funny story and then she told me her story. Her story began with her throwing a brick through a guy's living room window and another through his windshield. I was like "Okaaaaay." Now, I'm sure there was a reason behind her attack on his premises. I don't think it was a good idea, but something obviously provoked her to such rash actions. But perhaps she should've eased me into that story if she were going to tell it. Maybe giving the background on what led up to it first. Or, better yet, telling me the story after I'd had a chance to get to know her myself.

SHE HAS TOO MUCH DRAMA IN HER LIFE

There are two types of drama in life. The first is drama that is from circumstances beyond one's control that one's actively working to get beyond. The second is self-imposed drama. It's the self-imposed drama that becomes the problem. Some people fail miserably in making the cause-and-effect connection between their actions and the circumstances in their lives. Therefore, they live in drama.

The kind of bachelors who have a choice of women run from drama because they know drama queens are never satisfied unless there is tumult and upheaval going on all the time. Drama queens don't even recognize dramatics as problems; they see it as normal, and that drives away men who don't want to live that way.

SHE LACKS FOCUS OR GOALS FOR HER LIFE

I have a good friend who is an eligible bachelor who gets groom-o-phobia when he meets women who lack goals or focus for their lives. He's an educated professional man who desires a woman who is a deep thinker and goal-oriented person. He doesn't even require that a woman is already a professional or even a college graduate, as long as she's working toward such goals and has drive and determination. When he meets women who seem to be happily living a work-a-day lifestyle and have no plans for upward mobility, he's turned off.

SHE HAS A BAD REPUTATION

Hey, don't kill the messenger here. I'm not going to get into an argument about what's fair in judging the behavior of the genders. I'm just reporting what men say. Some things in this world have changed and some haven't. One thing that hasn't changed much is that men seem to want to have a good-time girl to fool around with, but want to marry a more traditional type they can take home to Mom. Just as in the old days, a bad reputation is something hard to overcome. When stories start surfacing about you, they can make it difficult, but not impossible, to get or maintain a relationship with some of the more sought-after men, at least where long-term relationships and marriage are concerned.

SHE'S LOOKING FOR A RELATIONSHIP THAT RESEMBLES A ROMANCE NOVEL

Men are by nature very pragmatic in their thinking. Even during that blissful romantic high that brings people together, we know there is going to be some hard work and long days to follow. So when we come across women who think it will all be happily ever after, a white picket fence, and a house on a hill, we get groom-o-phobia.

A tall and handsome eligible bachelor in Houston told me his story about being married to a woman who he now realizes was enchanted by his business reputation and fine home. They split when the romance novel reality ended after about a year of marriage. Once married, she began to resent the very things that attracted her to him: his strong work ethic, high-profile image, and frequent business travel. His work ethic often kept him up working late at night, even at home. And even her fantasies about business trips with him were not fulfilled because his out-of-town trips were often consumed with meetings, leaving him little time with her. He admits hindsight is better than foresight and says he should never have married her at all because he suspected she was marrying his image, not his real self.

SHE HAS A PSYCHOTIC EX HARASSING HER

I'll never forget a date I had with a girl whom I'll call Cheryl. Cheryl was a very attractive woman whom I met at a campaign fund-raiser for a city council member. We hit it off and had dinner one night. While at the restaurant, we decided to stop by the video store for a movie and go back to her condo. That's when things got interesting.

About halfway through the movie, I thought I heard the distinct sound of small rocks hitting her sliding glass door. Cheryl seemed not to be bothered, and since she was on the second level and it was past one in the morning, I dismissed the thought as my imagination. A few minutes later I bolted upright from her couch when I heard a large rock strike the glass. Cheryl got up without a word and marched to the kitchen and started boiling a big pot of water. I thought to myself, Has this woman gone mad? Meanwhile, another rock hit the window.

I eased over to the back door and saw a guy standing outside. When he saw me he started yelling and begging for Cheryl to come out on the balcony to talk to him. And she did go out on the balcony—but not to talk. She flung the hot water out over the railing and he ran. I could see that this wasn't an unusual situation for either of them. She went back into the kitchen and started boiling more water.

Shortly, we heard a banging on the door. He'd followed someone into the hallway of the building and was now screaming at the door. At the time, I was still a police officer and rarely went anywhere without a gun. I had a small pistol tucked in my boot and I was praying I wouldn't have to use it. Cheryl went to the door and started calming him down. He glared at me but eventually relaxed and finally left. Needless to say, after making sure the ranting and raving lunatic was gone, I left too.

Earlier I mentioned that a woman should not give a man groom-o-phobia by telling him too many things about her life up front. However, I made an exception for things that could endanger a person's health or safety, and this story illustrates why. Cheryl knew that her ex-husband was actively harassing her. I later found out more details about how he'd been following her and trying to sneak into her condo. Why she hadn't filed a protective order against him will always baffle me. However, the main point is that she didn't let me know and therefore placed me in danger without my knowledge.

THERE ARE TROUBLING ISSUES ABOUT HER CHILDREN

Okay, let's get one thing straight. In the twenty-first century, it's no big deal to meet women who have children already. For a man to say he isn't going to date women with kids would cut a number of really good prospects out of the picture.

But I'm going to explain to you the issue kids present from a bachelor's point of view.

He's Concerned About the Father Being a Problem

When getting involved with a woman who has children, a bachelor isn't as concerned about being a stepfather as he is about whether the biological father will be a problem. Will he try to be a physical threat? Will he pay his child support? Will he cause confusion in the children's lives?

He Doesn't Know If the Kids Are Well Disciplined

If children aren't well disciplined and respectful, they can give a man groom-o-phobia even if the woman doesn't. If, for example, the mother doesn't have a disciplinary grip on her kids, the prospective stepfather will be fighting an uphill battle to have authority in the house and gain the respect of the children.

The Children Have Special Needs

Who wants to marry a woman who has a child with emotional or behavioral issues? He has to be capable and prepared to deal with that situation before committing to being a husband and a stepfather. Children with special needs require a lot of energy and attention, and parenting them is not something that every stepfather can do.

Things to Think About

1. As a woman, what are your opinions about men having groom-o-phobia?
2. Based on the information in the chapter, is there anything women can do to ease the groom-o-phobia in men?
3. How can you differentiate a man who is a potentially good husband temporarily suffering from groom-o-phobia from a man who is simply not interested in marriage?

Journal Entry

What factors in your life or your personality do you think would give a potential husband groom-o-phobia?

Write an open letter to bachelors telling them how you feel about groom-o-phobia.

Inside the Mind of a Bachelor, Part 4

You see, it's already started. I had to get somebody else to play on our weekend basketball team Saturday because Eric couldn't make it. He had something to do with the family, he said. Like I told you before, next time I see the brother, he'll be balding and fat. How much do you want to bet his Corvette is already up for sale?

See, I'm not dissing my brother for getting married, because I know people fall in love and all. I'm sure one day even I'll want to settle down. But my problem is that I just can't deal with the thought of it all. It's too deep and serious.

I mean, think about it. Number one, I could never be with one woman for my entire life. Whew! That alone seems impossible. If I saw a really tight honey and she wanted to get with me, I'd have to be Mr. Noble and turn her down because I was married.

Number two is that a wife complicates things. You have to start planning everything, reporting in and making decisions you used to make on the fly—like how to spend your money. Everything becomes a committee decision. You have to discuss everything, from paying the light bill to which movie to rent from Blockbuster on Saturday night. I like my freedom.

Number three, and biggest of all, is the fact that when you get married, you don't really know what you're getting into. You think you do, but you really don't. I mean the divorce rate is like 50 percent. Do you think if those people knew their marriages would end in divorce one day that they would have gotten married in the first place? What makes me think I can make the right moves to get married successfully?

I don't know. I guess one day I'll see the light. But right now I can't understand being married and I don't want to. I wish Eric well.

5

What Does It Take for a Bachelor to Want to Become a Groom?

Like women, men have a basic need for intimacy. This is a human need, just as we need food, clothing, and shelter. It's just that some men don't discover their need for intimacy until they've made a roundabout journey. For some men, the realization comes naturally with maturity. For others, it's the result of soul searching. And some men even need to be shocked into realizing their need for intimacy after a traumatic episode in their lives.

There are essentially four things that comprise a man's decision to make the transformation from bachelor to married man:

1. He's ready to make the transition.
2. He must feel at ease with his woman.

3. He must feel there's a mutual benefit to the relationship.
4. He feels he's had his "run."

Unless these four issues have been satisfied, a man isn't ready to cross the bridge from bachelorhood to marriage. Summarizing these issues is easy, but they are more complicated than meets the eye. Let's look at each in more detail.

He Feels He's Ready

There's a time when every man who is destined for marriage is ready for marriage. There is an alarm clock that goes off inside his head that nobody can hear but him. Contrary to popular belief, it's not related to his age or to pressures from his woman or family. It's because he feels it's time. He feels ready and prepared to move into that phase of his life.

Of course, this isn't to say that men don't get married everyday just because they're turning thirty, their families feel that they should be married, or they are getting pressured by their women, because they do—with varying results following those pressured decisions. But actually, the optimal time for a man to get married is when he feels it is time.

So how does he know it's time? The answer to this question is strictly individual. But two universal factors can be isolated as things that a man feels are necessary before he can say he's ready to get married: economic stability and the need for intimacy.

A man must feel that he's economically able to fulfill the role of provider and protector. Of course, today's provider and protector role is more about having a career and health and retirement benefits for one's family than it is about fending off villains with a shotgun. But if need be, a man wants to feel he is capable of doing that too.

BEING
Ready's
Mean ➔ A man must also have a need for authentic and genuine companionship or intimacy that he can't fulfill by playing the field. This is a critical point for a bachelor to reach. In a sense, he comes full circle and realizes that he isn't going to find what he's looking for between the sheets or by dating multiple women.

BRIAN: PLAYING HOUSE, BUT NOT READY TO TAKE THE PLUNGE

I know I sound like every other guy when I say I'm not ready. But I'm just not ready. I do love my girlfriend and she's the only one, but marriage is a big step that I can't handle yet. I have a job that isn't a career, it's just a job. I struggle to make ends meet by myself, so supporting the two of us would be impossible, plus you know she'd want to have a baby too. To be honest, I'm frustrated right now and not very happy with my life at this point. I want to go back to school to finish my degree and get a good job. I don't want to try to do all that, work, and be married too.

Yet my girlfriend is always talking about us getting married. We've been together four years and she thinks it's time. When I tell her I'm not ready, her favorite thing to say is that I should be able to "walk and chew gum at the same time." She believes in that "we can struggle and make it together" fantasy bull. But I don't want to struggle. I'd rather just keep arguing with her than to get married before I'm ready.

JULIUS: FEELING SOCIAL PRESSURE THAT HE SHOULD BE MARRIED

I'm turning forty in a few months and I've never been married. I've had some close relationships, but none of them panned out. In one case, my girl left me for another guy after a three-year relationship. The second big love of my life decided she wanted to move to another state for a new job offer. We were together a year before she moved. Then we tried the long-distance thing, but it didn't work for us and we drifted apart after another year. The third girl I thought I was going to marry was someone I realized that I was just trying to make myself love because she seemed so right for me on the outside. But inside I knew I didn't love her. I loved the idea of us being married and having a family. The day I went to buy a ring for her I couldn't make myself do it. It also helped that I had a really bad stomachache that day. I figured it was a sign. That relationship was about a year of my life.

Now here I am pushing forty. I'm single, I have no kids, and I feel that I should be married and have kids like most of my friends. The only friend I have who isn't married and has no kids is that way because he's divorced. Well, then, of course, I have another buddy who's an artist, a real character. He's not attached and has no kids. But marriage is not his style.

It can be depressing to think about. I feel like it's time, but I have no real prospects. My folks want grandchildren, and they really give me a hard time about it, especially my dad. I think my mom knows I don't just want to marry someone under false pretenses and then get a divorce. But my dad thinks I just ought to go out and get a good healthy girl pregnant so I'll at least have a kid. He tells me to just have a kid and not to get married. Go figure.

He Must Feel at Ease with His Woman

There's a term that all men understand when rating a woman: that is whether or not she's cool. When a guy says this to his friends to describe a woman's attitude and his feelings about her, he's giving her the ultimate compliment. By saying "She's cool," he's really saying "I can feel at ease around her. I don't feel that I have to play the traditional male-female games with her. I can be myself with her. She likes me for who I am."

Following is a list of the traits of a "cool" woman:

1. She isn't a high-maintenance mate.
2. She isn't a drama queen.
3. She doesn't try to keep tabs on a man by calling and paging him all the time.
4. She doesn't cross-examine him about the details of everything he says or does.
5. She has a peaceful and calming effect on his life.
6. She makes him feel masculine.
7. He finds her sexually exciting.

But there's a caveat. A woman who's seen as cool can become an accidental gal pal if she isn't careful. This is akin to the way a man can become a buddy or like a brother to a woman with whom he wants a relationship. The accidental gal pal's mistake is that when she has an opportunity to get the man she wants, she doesn't assert that she's interested in more than being friends. Let's take Linda, for example.

LINDA: THE ACCIDENTAL GAL PAL WHO WANTED TO BE MORE

I have a crush on a friend of mine. This isn't something that has just developed. I've felt this way for some time now. We met at a mutual friend's party. It rained really hard that night because there was a tropical storm approaching so only a few people showed up. But instead of it being dead, the seven of us that showed had a blast. Anyway, this guy, Steve, was so sweet that he went out of his way to give me a ride home in that bad storm. He was cute, but also had just started seeing someone, so I didn't go after him.

Two weeks later, I'm at an Astros game and who do I bump into? Steve, of course. Now, this is odd because I don't even go to baseball games. I just went because our company gave us tickets. He bought me a beer and we talked. He told me the girl he was dating wasn't working out and he said he was glad this happened early, after only a month, before he got too attached. I felt bad for him because he was so sweet. But I was jumping for joy inside because I saw a chance to get him myself. This time I got his number.

The first night we talked we were on the phone for hours. We had great chemistry, and I know I wasn't the only one feeling that way. Mostly we talked about his old relationships, and I was counseling him with a woman's perspective on things. Steve and I talked on the phone for weeks and I really felt he'd be ready to start dating me soon. Especially since he wasn't in a serious relationship with the girl he'd just stopped seeing. But, boy, was I wrong. Steve started going out with his friends and even inviting me along to hang out with them. I went along a few times and that's when I realized Steve saw me as just one of the boys. He even started asking me for advice about women he was meeting and dating. I was completely overlooked as a potential girlfriend.

He Must Feel There's Mutual Benefit in the Relationship

A man wants to feel useful and important to his woman. The need for men to be needed could offer some explanation of the marriage gradient theory, as explained in J. Bernard's *The Future of Marriage,* which suggests that American men tend to marry women who are younger, smaller in stature, and have a lower income or social status than they do (and vice versa for women). The marriage gradient theory is a general picture of the situation, and every day men and women defy the odds. However, the fact that it tends to be true is troubling in that some prevailing social beliefs, such as the ideas that cause this behavior, tend to inhibit God only knows how many great potential couples from forming. My advice to both men and women is to defy the odds, keep an open mind, and see what you discover out there!

Actually, many modern bachelors want their women to provide significant input to the relationship. They don't want to marry women who aren't going to bring something to the table other than just looks and a great body. Sure, when guys are just dating around, it's all about a woman's body and looks, but when they're looking for a real relationship, other things start weighing in heavily. Factors such as income, education, and background become important. Let's take George, for example.

GEORGE: MARRYING MUTUALLY

George said he didn't wake up one day and just decide he was going to marry a doctor. Instead, it was something that happened as a result of the environment he found himself a part of for years.

> *In med school the only people you ever see are your classmates, and that's how we met. There aren't a lot of people who can understand the pressures of med school and the schedule. But since Allison was also in medical school with me, she could relate. Our toughest time was during our residencies because of the crazy schedule. But as I said, we already expected this because we were both doctors.*

I asked George if income potential factored into his decision to marry a doctor.

> *Yes and no. I do like the fact that she will eventually have a high income. That will allow us to achieve a lot more in life. It also means that I don't have to carry the load on everything. But I didn't marry her M.D. degree. If Allison wasn't a match for me, her income potential wouldn't have made me marry her because I'll eventually make plenty of money myself. At the same time, it helps that she doesn't need money from me so I also feel she didn't have to marry me just because I'm a doctor.*

I also asked George how important he felt it was that people marry mutually.

I think it's important to marry someone on the same page with you. In other words, they don't have to be exactly like you in education or profession, but they need to be on the same page when it comes to the important things. People think Allison and I are a match just because we're both doctors. But that's not the whole picture. I believe that does help us understand each other better. But most important, when it comes down to the essential things that it takes to make a relationship work, like communication, trust, and respect, we're in agreement.

He Feels He's Had His Run

When we were single (most of my friends are married now), we used to refer to marriage as retiring. Meaning that after a bachelor has had his fill of the world of wine, women, and song, he'd be ready to move on. Sort of the way a person doesn't want to eat another bite once he's full. This is a very important point to consider because it has a lot of truth to it. I've seen more than one man get married and lament that he'd never sown his wild oats.

I'm not saying that I think a bachelor should go sleep with half the women in the city before feeling he's had his run. I'm speaking in terms of him having felt the autonomy and freedom he needs to feel before moving on to the next stage in life. For example, I know of one bachelor whose feeling that he'd had his run was evidenced by the fact that he wanted to live alone in his own apartment with no roommates. For him it was about a sense of freedom. Sure, for a lot of men, it's about being a superstud. But I say if they can't harness that urge, it's better for them to express it before marriage than after.

DANNY: I MISSED OUT!

Danny's e-mail told the story of a man living with secret desires. He's a good man who seemed to be a great husband. Yet not very far underneath it all, he has an insatiable curiosity about other women. He was married a year after graduation from college to his college sweetheart whom he'd been with since his freshman year. During the time they were together in college, they broke up a couple of times and both dated others, but never for too long. Now Danny finds himself in his mid-twenties, married, with a new son. Meanwhile, his college friends are switching into the next gear of full-fledged bachelorhood. He is the only guy in his group of friends who's married and the only one who's a father. He feels that he's missing out because while he's at home "feeling domesticated," as he puts it, his friends are out living it up all over town and dating all sorts of beautiful women. Only time will tell if Danny grows into a realization and appreciation of what he has with his wife, or if he'll have to take the longer route of learning the hard way. Regardless of what happens, his story illustrates one of the important points about bachelorhood being a rite of passage in itself.

Things to Think About

1. What role does a woman play in a man's desire to change from bachelor to married man?
2. What is a healthy and nondestructive way for a bachelor to have his run?
3. How does succumbing to social pressure to marry affect a man's feelings in a marriage?

Journal Exercise

Consider the idea of cool women as presented in this chapter. List the things that make you a cool woman. Include examples. If you don't feel men think of you this way, write about why they may not have that opinion of you.

Have you ever been an accidental gal pal? How did you get into that position? What did you do? How can you keep it from happening again?

Inside the Mind of a Bachelor, Part 5

Well, I did call Nancy after all. We even went out last weekend. That's right, on a real date, not a booty call. We went to the park last Sunday and then had lunch at a little bistro next to the lake. It was really nice.

Turns out I have already started finding the right buttons

to push on her control panel. She didn't come right out and say it, but whether she knows it or not, she told me enough for me to figure out that she's lonely and badly wants a meaningful relationship. And if I know one thing, I know lonely women are usually horny women because they have all of that passionate energy just bottled up waiting to explode.

But you know what? I'm not even going there with her, and that's what scares me. I'm not saying watching that honey brown ass in those white shorts didn't stir my loins, because it did. But I was actually enjoying talking and chilling with her too. And that scares me because the number-one way a man knows he really likes a woman is when his first thought about her isn't about getting her into the sack.

Nancy doesn't do any of the things that usually scare me off from relationships. Another thing I like about her is that she's realistic. She's not expecting some dude to scoop her up on a white stallion to a castle on a hill. She's not one of those women who wants to sit at home while I work my ass off either. She has her own career and goals. She's a pharmacist like Cindy; that's how they know each other. And it's really relaxing to be with her. I don't even feel like I have to act like I'm on a date when I'm with her.

As I said, she's really cool too. I really felt comfortable with her. We didn't even need any entertainment. You know how sometimes when you go out with someone, you have to go to a movie because you don't really feel comfortable talking to them. Well, with Nancy, we went to the park, shared some popcorn, and the rest of the date was just walking and talking, feeding the ducks, and watching kids play on the swings. I can't believe I'm talking like this. But with Nancy, I don't feel the same way I feel with other girls I know. Nancy is different. If I was going to be married, it would be with a woman like her.

Anyway, I'm trippin', talking about marriage and all that stuff.

6

How to Read a Bachelor

Men are not subtle creatures. We always telegraph our thoughts and feelings. But women usually just don't know what signs to watch for. Nowhere is that more evident than in the dating world, particularly for those women who are interested in finding marital partners among bachelors who are often reluctant or more interested in remaining married to their bachelorhood than to a woman.

For women to better understand what they're dealing with, they must first know how to read a bachelor. A woman who's interested in finding a long-term relationship or a husband doesn't need to waste her time with men who aren't seeking the same.

Basically, bachelors can be divided into four categories:

1. Marriage minded: those who are serious about wanting a long-term relationship leading to marriage.
2. Men in transition: men who are in the limbo that comes after being a player, but before deciding to seek a commitment.
3. Players: those who are not at all interested in relationships.
4. Wildcards: men who shift from being marriage minded, players, and men in development, depending on circumstances at the time.

Though all bachelors tend to fall into these categories, they aren't mutually exclusive; a man could have characteristics of more than one type.

Marriage-minded Bachelors

Marriage-minded bachelors are men who have already decided their next step in life is to find a good wife. They could have reached this stage in their lives by growing tired of being players or by realizing that they were ready to be married. Also included in this category is the rare man who forgoes the games of bachelorhood and immediately begins seeking a wife.

The marriage-minded bachelor tends to be in a stable career. He also tends to be self-confident and focused. This man sees getting married as a progression, not as a loss of himself or his freedom. He's looking forward to marriage and is actively seeking a mate.

Men in Transition

These are bachelors in a transitional stage, somewhere between the exploration stage and the conversion stage mentioned in Chapter 2 (see pages 25–26). These are men who are on their way to becoming marriage-minded men. They can be found at various stages in life. Some are naive college boys who are only beginning to learn about relationships. Some are divorced men who've been tempered in life's fire and now know what they really want in a relationship. Others are men of mature age who may be transitioning after the death of a spouse or a divorce late in life. Despite outward differences, men who fall into this category share one thing in common: They're all learning about what it takes to be successful in a relationship. Often they're on the cusp of beginning a long-term relationship or marriage. However, they haven't yet become absolutely comfortable with the idea of being in a relationship. Finally, men in development differ from wildcards because these men do in fact know that they want to be marriage-minded men.

Players

We know the characteristics of players. Basically, they're the opposite of the marriage-minded bachelors. Players actively avoid committed relationships. They think with the brain in their pants, not with the one in their heads. They're busy living the bachelor high life of wine, women, and song.

It's worth mentioning that just because players are hedonistic doesn't mean they're screw-ups. Players come in all forms and in every socioeconomic category. Some live at home with their moms, and some have luxury homes in three cities. Being a player is more of a mind-set than it is a station in life, and that's important to remember when reading bachelors. The outside doesn't tell you the content of a man's character. For a more detailed discussion of players, refer to Chapter 8, "How to Avoid Being Played by the Players."

Wildcards

Wildcards are perhaps the most intriguing bachelors because they can't be easily identified, and, depending on the circumstances, they change. They share common characteristics both with marriage-minded bachelors and with players.

Wildcards aren't fully sure of what they want. As a result of the wildcard's indecision, he is likely to become a player when he's around women who are not looking for more than a good time. But when put into a situation with a marriage-minded woman, the wildcard becomes interested in a long-term relationship leading to marriage. It's not that he's not capable of following through on being one way or the other; he's just the easily influenced type. In a sense, he can be molded, like clay, although he may not remain in the form in which he's molded. He may be a potential risk in a long-term relationship or marriage.

Now that you know the categories, let's look at some of the various forms bachelors assume within each category.

How to Recognize and Read the Common Types of Bachelors

Boy-Toy Bachelor

Categories: Player, wildcard
Clothing: High fashion, designer
Speech: Latest slang
Habitat: Popular nightclubs, trendy restaurants, entertainment events, and concerts
Characteristics: This is the guy who makes the ladies swoon. He's eye candy. He's cute, fun, and wild. But he often lacks the ability to be dependable or to follow through. Also, you always get this sneaking suspicion about him, the feeling that something's not right, but you just can't put your finger on it.

Good-Man Bachelor

Categories: Marriage-minded Bachelor, Wildcard, Man in Transition

Clothing: Conservative

Speech: Proper diction and good grammar

Habitat: Quiet, settled neighborhoods; grocery stores; and civic, volunteer, and political events (Note: He doesn't go out to clubs or parties much.)

Characteristics: This is the honest-to-goodness man you take home to Mom. He's clean cut, honest, and sincere. He has great manners. He's a hardworking man who wants to have a wife and family. He is the proverbial old-fashioned guy.

Politically Correct Bachelor

Categories: Marriage-minded Bachelor, Wildcard, Man in Transition

Clothing: Conservative

Speech: Proper diction and good grammar

Habitat: Upscale neighborhoods; popular restaurants; and social and political events

Characteristics: The politically correct bachelor is educated and has a solid career. He tends to be stable, but not necessarily boring. He's interesting and fun too. However, sometimes politically correct bachelors are wild men in disguise. He's similar to the good-man bachelor, except he's more likely to change with trends.

Carnal Bachelor

Category: Player
Clothing: Fashion, Street
Speech: Slang
Habitat: Popular nightclubs, trendy restaurants,
entertainment events, and concerts
Characteristics: This is the seductive man who
appeals to your lowest carnal desires. He tempts
you to compromise your values, morals, and ethics.
He's no good for you. Yet you still find yourself
drawn into his world by some magnetism that he
has. Be careful; this one's the devil with blue
jeans on.

Bad-Boy Bachelor

Categories: Player, Wildcard
Clothing: High fashion
Speech: Slang
Habitat: Popular nightclubs, trendy restaurants,
entertainment events, and concerts
Characteristics: He's similar to the Carnal Bachelor,
but not as dangerous. He is cute and lots of fun.
He's like a mixture between a precocious little boy
and a rottweiler. But the truth is that he's
immature and not planning on growing up anytime
soon. Maybe it's that quality that makes him
irresistible. With just a little work, he'd be a good

man. But he isn't planning on changing, and you can't change him. That's why he's a bad boy and not a bad man.

Common Mistakes in Reading and Trying to Influence Bachelors

Following is a list of the most common mistakes women make when attempting to read or influence bachelors.

1. Assuming men will see things the way women do

Probably the biggest mistake women make is trying to figure out bachelors in terms of the way women think. Women often ask me "Doesn't he know what he's missing?" Or "How could he want the kind of woman he left me for?" What they don't realize is that men don't think the same way women do, and they never will!

2. Believing his words over his actions

Many bachelors say one thing but do another. A typical example is the guy who says, "I'm looking for a relationship." But he has a little black book full of numbers and he's dating two or three different women every week. His actions don't say he wants a relationship. Then there's the guy who claims he wants a relationship, but he's not putting in the time and effort it takes to develop one. Obviously, his actions are speaking more clearly than his words, and that's what women need to judge by.

3. Thinking too far ahead

It's a mistake to get too far ahead of a bachelor in a relationship. For example, some women meet men who appear to be on their way to becoming successful in life and attempt to stake a claim early. Their strategy, in a sense, is to reserve that man for later, when he's ready to get into a relationship or a marriage. They attempt to achieve this by various methods. But the goal is to leave an indelible impression of themselves on his mind. This is a flawed strategy. Timing is of utmost importance in relationships. Getting in good with him today doesn't necessarily ensure anything for tomorrow.

4. Judging men solely on their type, not as individuals

In college, a friend of mine was totally infatuated with a guy she thought was on his way to becoming a success in life. After all, he fit the profile. He was from a well-known family. He was smart, well spoken, handsome, and a fraternity man. But there was one problem with him: He had no ambition whatsoever. He made it through a few years of college, decreasing his course load as he went. Soon his only campus activities were showing up for Greek shows and parties. Finally he quit altogether. My friend finally got the message that he wasn't going anywhere. She'd learned a lesson. She made the mistake of being in love with what he could be, not with who he was.

How to Know If He's Serious About You

Ah, that dreaded question: Is he serious? Instead of agonizing over it, use this checklist to get a clear picture of the answer.

1. He will have healthy disagreements with you.
A man who's serious about a relationship will react to disagreements in a healthy way. In other words, every time there's an argument or disagreement, he won't be ready simply to walk out the door. He'll be willing to talk about things, work things out, and seek solutions together.

2. He will prioritize time with you.
Everybody's busy these days. Anyone should be allowed to be late for a date here and there. But I don't care if a man is a sanitation worker or the mayor; he'll make time for a woman he loves. Men are empowered in a way words can't describe by the presence of a good woman in their lives. And when they find a woman who is a great complement to

their lives, they will go to great lengths to be with her.

3. *He will introduce you to his friends and family.*
If a bachelor doesn't introduce you to his friends and family voluntarily, he's not serious about you. A man will *always* introduce a woman he loves to his friends and family. He wants them to see her because he's proud of her. He wants them to share in his joy about having this woman in his life. Of course, this creates no guarantee for the relationship, but it is a strong sign of good intentions.

4. *He will take you to events important to his life.*
In addition to introducing a woman to his family and friends, a man will take a woman he loves to events that are important and meaningful to his life. This is because he wants her energy to be a part of things that are significant to him. As stated in number 3, this is not in itself a guarantee for the relationship, but it is a good sign that a woman has been taken into a deeper place in his life.

5. *He will feel at ease around you.*
If a bachelor is totally at ease around you, you're really getting close to his heart because this means he feels you're cool. (Refer to Chapter 5, "What Does It Take for a Bachelor to Want to Become a Groom?," page 72, for more on what makes a cool woman.) When a man really feels he can be himself with a

woman, he's probably found the woman he's going to marry.

6. He doesn't consider you one of the boys.
You want a man to feel totally at ease around you, but you still want him to treat you like a lady, with respect and dignity. That's where this last issue comes in. When a man loves you, though he feels comfortable with you, you're still his lady. He still honors you and respects you. He still acts like a gentleman toward you and doesn't take you for granted or act lewd or obnoxious with you.

Things to Think About

1. How accurate is the outward appearance of a person as a gauge of the kind of person he or she actually is?
2. What role do your expectations play in the way you perceive the men you meet as compared to what they are really telling you with their actions?
3. What are some types and categories of bachelorettes that you can think of?

Journal Exercise

Have you ever been really interested in a man but later found out he was a totally different person from what you'd anticipated? What first impressions made you think he was the type of man you thought he was, instead of the type of man he actually was? Was it his looks, speech, profession, his clothing, or maybe his car?

Reflect on some things you can do to get to know a man better for who he actually is instead of typecasting him based on his external appearance.

Inside the Mind of a Bachelor, Part 6

You know, I admit to being a player; well, I guess I'm a reformed player nowadays. But even though I was a player, some of the women played themselves. I mean really, if they just would've read the way I acted versus what I said, they'd have known where I was coming from and what I was really about.

For instance, a girl named Linda that I was dating thought we were a couple, but we weren't. I guess she wanted a boyfriend so badly that she just claimed me. I never did anything to make her think she was my girl. In fact, I stood her up for two dates in a row and she still overlooked that. Then there was Allison. She just didn't want to hear the truth. I told her I didn't want a relationship. But she thought just because I had a degree and wore a suit to work every day that I would make a good husband for her. I tried to tell her that once I took off the suit, I was a baller, not a yuppie. So it's not always the man who plays the woman; some of these women play themselves without any help.

On the other hand, there's the way I treat Nancy. I

mean, she could have no doubt that I'm into her. I'm always spending time with her. I've introduced her to my best friends. We've been to parties with my coworkers, and I definitely wouldn't take just anyone around those snooty hoity-toity people. I even took her to dinner with my mom and dad. To tell you the truth, it all surprised me because I just found myself doing these things naturally with her. All a woman has to do if she wants to know what she means to a man is to pay attention to how he treats her. How's his attitude toward her? What priority does she get in his life? Is she more important to him than other women? The answers to these simple questions tell a whole lot. When I thought about these questions in terms of Nancy, I realized I was in deep. I think I'm in love . . . and I like it.

7

How to Sift Through
All the Game Players
to Find Mr. Right

From an ex-bachelor's perspective, I can tell you that you can increase your odds of meeting the right man significantly by applying a few simple ideas to your search. If you apply the ideas I give you in this chapter, I guarantee that you'll meet more bachelors who meet your standards.

Finding the right mate is a very important spiritual pursuit. Sadly, I think our society has trivialized this pursuit, and that's part of the reason people are finding the wrong mates. Remember, finding a mate is not a contest to win or a game to play, it's one of the most important things you'll ever do, and it affects all aspects of your life.

The Three Elements of Meeting a Mr. Right

There are basically three factors involved in meeting the right type of man for you:

1. Knowing yourself well enough to make a good choice
2. Using smart methods to your advantage
3. Keeping an open mind and having fun

KNOW YOURSELF

Last year I was watching an episode of the *Oprah* show, "Women Who Rock!" One of the women featured was Jada Pinkett Smith, an actor and wife of actor Will Smith. I loved what Jada said about her relationship with Will. She emphasized the fact that to attract an eligible bachelor, she first had to become the kind of person she wanted to attract. She also said that as a couple, not only do they work at improving their relationship, but they work at improving themselves as individuals too. The key to a relationship is two whole people coming together to form something bigger—not, as the myth suggests, two half people coming together to make one.

What Jada said was absolutely on target. The only way to find the whole bachelor you are looking for is to make good decisions about the men you become involved with, and the only way you can do so is to do the homework it takes to become relatively centered and at peace before getting into a relationship. This is important because you're in no state of mind to assess others until you really have a good idea of who you are. Otherwise, your unconscious issues will continue to drive all of the decisions in your life, including the men you choose to be involved with. Think about it.

GIVE YOURSELF THE ADVANTAGE

To connect with the right man for you, you have to work smarter, not harder. Instead of believing that the right man is going to happen to come along, you have to get proactive in your search. Some say they'll let fate take care of arranging their meeting with Mr. Right. Well, to those women I say, That's fine, but fate's methods frequently can be upgraded with technology! This chapter highlights several methods for meeting men that can increase your pool of contacts with eligible bachelors while allowing you maximum screening ability to separate the champs from the chumps.

ENJOY YOURSELF

Always remember to relax and have fun. If you're living and loving yourself, other people are drawn to you automatically. Confident, purposeful women draw men who are of the same fabric, and they repel weak men (the kind they don't want anyway). So don't go on a husband hunt. Don't get overly intense, anxious, or apprehensive. Instead, have some fun with dating and meeting men.

How to Meet the Right Type of Man for You

More than likely, Mr. Right isn't just going to walk up and introduce himself saying "Hey, it's me. Mr. Right!" Nor is there a man out there walking around with a flashing neon sign on his head with your name on it saying "Here I am, Angela. Just for you!" Instead, the truth of the matter is that everyday you're walking right by the right types of men. You are standing next to them on crowded subway trains and even sitting next to them at the movies while you're on a date with Mr. Wrong.

This chapter is for women who are truly ready to meet the right man to marry but are wondering how to play an active role in the process. It's for women who don't believe that there will be a puff of smoke out of which the perfect husband will appear. For two right people to meet, they have to have the right situation to bring them together at the right time and place. Obviously in a world of over 6 billion people (and counting), that's a seemingly impossible—at the very least improbable—task. Yet everyday people who are the right types for each other meet. How? Actually, in all sorts of ways. It could be something as simple as a casual chance encounter at the grocery store or something as seemingly improbable as a fender bender in a mall parking lot. There are introductions made by friends, meetings at work, and dating services. The possibilities are endless. I think one of the funniest stories I know of was a police officer who pulled a woman over for a ticket and ended up marrying her.

Unfortunately, some people believe you should just sit and wait for the right person to come along. But those people are waiting for something that may or may not happen. You don't wait for a college degree, you *make* it happen. You don't wait for the right job, you send out résumés and go to interviews. People don't seem to expect any great and important experience in life to just happen, except this one. But that's not a good strategy for a decision that is probably the most critical you will ever make and will affect each and every aspect of your life.

That's why you should make a serious effort to meet the right type of man for you. Not a desperate search, but an effort that opens you up to a greater probability of meeting a man who is the right type for you. This isn't about being desperate. There's a big difference between being desperate and being smart. Being desperate is mindlessly chasing each man you meet without the slightest clue as to whether you may be compatible with him. Being smart, however, is putting yourself in a position in which you can meet more eligible men. A popular adage defines insanity as trying the same thing over and over and expecting a different result. I don't know who said it first, but it's true, especially when it comes to the search for the right mate. Too many women who are searching for a husband and not finding him continue to use the same methods, not realizing that if years of trying haven't produced him, perhaps they are better off with a different approach.

MEETING THE RIGHT MAN ISN'T A SCIENTIFIC PROCESS

Although I'm talking about using different approaches to meet the right man in a methodical and logical way, I don't want to imply that this is a scientific process, because it's not. People aren't lab rats with predictable traits and characteristics, we're spirits, and that's where our connection ultimately has to be anchored for any marriage to be successful. It's not my intention to make it look as if you can sit in front of your computer and the right man will simply pop up on the screen. Or that you can run a personal ad and an absolutely ideal man will call the next day. Nor is this discounting the reality that people just meet each other every day while walking down the street, jogging, or at work. There is no single perfect way to meet someone. But from the experiences of my bachelor days, I can tell you that there are some definite advantages and pitfalls to different ways of meeting.

DISPEL THE MYTH OF THE ONE FOR YOU

Before you delve into increasing your pool of eligible men, dispel the myth of "the one." This is probably one of the most dangerous and anxiety-producing beliefs a single person can have, especially single women. There *isn't* just one person for you, some man who's your missing half in the over 6 billion people on earth. The truth is that there's a right *type* of man for you, and many men may fit that type.

I definitely believe in soul mates. But a soul mate is about finding a kindred type of spirit more than it is about finding a specific individual.

The Ten Ways to Meet Your Mr. Right

The following is my method of evaluating the ten ways to meet your Mr. Right, which are meeting men online, dating services, personals ads, singles' events, singles' events sponsored by religious organizations, volunteer activities, parties, friends of friends, the Aunt Sally introduction, and casual intersections. These ways are rated in the following ways: expense, con factor, time required, and stress.

EXPENSE

Meeting men by some of the following methods will require an amount of financial investment. The amount of that investment depends on the methods you use to meet men. Some methods, such as personal ads, are relatively inexpensive. Others, such as dating services, can be costly.

Expense Rating Scale

1 = The cost of going dutch with a date for coffee and dessert.
2 = The cost of paying for dinner and a movie on a date.

3 = Something that will make a dent in your monthly budget.

CON FACTOR

There's always the chance that a man you meet isn't being straight with you. Maybe he's not really looking for a relationship. Perhaps he isn't at all the way he describes himself to be. Or perhaps he says he's unattached but actually has a girlfriend, a wife, or both! No matter what the method, there's always a chance of being conned.

Con Factor Rating Scale

1 = It's easy to get an idea of the type of person he really is.

2 = You could be easily deceived in the beginning, but less so over time.

3 = You could be totally hoodwinked.

TIME REQUIRED

Just as you must invest some money in the methods to meet men, you must also invest time. The amount of time needed to start meeting quality eligible men will vary with the method used. For example, from my experience, meeting women through a dating service was one of the most time-efficient ways to meet eligible women. In contrast, meeting women by the Aunt Sally method would've taken much longer.

Time Required Rating Scale

---

1 = A few hours per month.

2 = A few hours per week.

3 = An hour or two daily.

STRESS

Some of the methods can really put you on the spot by requiring you to improvise quick, witty conversation, risk getting the cold shoulder, or endure a long date with a mismatch. On the other hand, several of the methods give you the opportunity of getting acquainted with a man (or getting general information about him) from a comfortable distance.

Stress Rating Scale

---

1 = Minimal stress (butterflies in the stomach, little jitters).

2 = Anxiety equivalent to asking for a date.

3 = Can potentially create high anxiety and apprehension.

Rating and Comments on Each Method

MEETING MEN ONLINE

Expense: Some on-line dating clubs are free, most are no more than the cost of going dutch with a date for coffee and dessert.

Dupe Factor: You could be totally hoodwinked.

Time: A few hours per week.

Stress: Little or low stress involved.

The upside of meeting men through online dating services and singles forums is that the Internet allows you a wall of anonymity behind which you can remain at a safe distance while getting to know him. But that wall can also have a downside. It can provide a player with an easy way to shield his true tendencies from you. When using this method, you'll have to endure the suspense of wondering if he's being truthful about everything and if he really looks like that photo he e-mailed you or posted on the web.

DATING SERVICES

Expense: Something that will make a dent in your monthly budget.

Dupe Factor: It's easy to get an idea of the type of man he is.

Time: A few hours per week.

Stress: Little or low stress involved.

Overall, dating services are by far the most efficient means of meeting men, but good ones tend to be expensive. When I was single, I tried a nationally known dating service for about a year. They had a plush living room–style office suite with a library full of personal profiles, photos, videos, and computer terminals all for the purpose of searching for the right match. While a member there, I learned that some of the photos weren't that reliable because some of the women had glamour shots instead of everyday snapshots. The profiles were most important to me because they were in a biographical format with standard questions. It was interesting to see how some women answered with one or two bland sentences, and others had short paragraphs full of interesting things to say. I also found the videos very useful because I could listen to a woman's voice inflections, read her body language, and get a better gut feeling about her.

Basically, the service I was a member of had a simple method. I looked through the library for women who matched my desired characteristics, read their profiles, and looked at their photos. Then I watched their videos in a private cubicle. If I felt an attraction to one of the women, or even two or three, I'd leave a message with the service and they would make the contact. Then the woman could check out my bio, photos, and video. If she wanted to meet, they'd hook us up. If not, she simply declined. It was totally efficient. No awkward stares across crowded rooms. No "I wonder if she's married or has a boyfriend" thoughts. No need to think of a way to ask for a phone number or a date. And best of all, no cracked face from being insulted.

PERSONAL ADS

Expense: Free or, the cost of going dutch with a date for coffee and dessert.

Dupe Factor: You could be easily deceived at the beginning, but less with time.

Time: A few hours per week.

Stress: Anxiety equivalent to asking for a date.

I think personal ads, especially those that combine a printed ad with a voice mail feature, are a great way to meet someone. You can learn a lot about a person from his voice. Tonal inflections, diction, and other nuances all combine to create a mental picture of a person's attitude and general personality. But remember, at around two bucks a minute, the cost of phone calls to respond to the ads can add up quickly. However, if you set reasonable limits for yourself, you won't rack up lots of expense making or retrieving calls. Limit the number of calls you will make and how much you will spend. Most important, be sure first to spend ample time on the telephone talking to the men you've met before arranging face-to-face meetings. (Important note: See "First-Date Essentials" section of this chapter.) You need to know whether there's enough interest to even have a meeting or first date; that's the whole purpose of using personal ads— to meet men you have the most compatibility with. Though this method is a great sifter, it still builds some anxiety, and you'll probably have some apprehension about the first meeting. Is he what he described himself to be? Will he think you're too short, too fat, or too something or other?

SINGLES' EVENTS

Expense: The cost of going dutch with a date for coffee and dessert.

Dupe Factor: You could be easily deceived at the beginning, but less with time.

Time: A few hours per month.

Stress: Anxiety equivalent to asking for a date.

Singles' events can be a lot of fun if they have lots of people and are well coordinated. But without good planning they can be boring and intimidating. When I was single I attended both types of events. Good events featured some sort of entertainment, a light buffet, and at least one type of activity designed to break the ice or act as a people mixer. But the poorly planned events simply ended up being a room full of people who gravitated toward clusters of people they knew; in the worst-case scenario, I found myself walking around with a name tag on sipping an overpriced glass of Coke and trying not to look like the kid who didn't get chosen for either team in a kickball game.

SINGLES' EVENTS SPONSORED BY RELIGIOUS ORGANIZATIONS

Expense: Free or the cost of going dutch with a date for coffee and dessert.

Dupe Factor: You could be easily deceived in the beginning, but less with time.

Time: A few hours per week.

Stress: Anxiety equivalent to asking for a date.

Churches and religious organizations have always been meeting places for singles. In fact, you can use sitting alone during services week after week as a deliberate signal to women that you're available. Since the membership of various churches is often focused on groups of people with the same styles and tastes, churches and other places of worship can be great places to meet someone with common interests. However, the drawback to dating someone from your church, synagogue, or mosque, especially if it's a small one, is the likelihood that everyone will be in your personal business. For example, in a small church, if you're seen flirting with a man for three or four weeks, then suddenly you two don't even speak the next week, you could become choir practice gossip. This probably isn't such an issue in larger churches with thousands of members and several services on Sunday. I also want to give out a word to the wise about meeting men in church. Be realistic and level-headed about them just as you would about any other men. Just because you meet a man at church (or a religious organization's function) doesn't mean he's going to behave like a saint!

VOLUNTEER ACTIVITIES

Expense: Free or the cost of going dutch with a date for coffee and dessert.

Dupe Factor: You could be easily deceived in the beginning, but less with time.

Time: A few hours per month (possibly more depending on your involvement).

Stress: Anxiety equivalent to asking for a date.

The good thing about volunteer activities is that they take the focus off of meeting someone and place it on something else, such as being a mentor, repairing an elderly person's home, picking up trash in the park, or helping your favorite political candidate. Thus, through engaging in a particular activity with eligible single men, you're able to talk, laugh, and interact in a way that is likely to reveal a lot more about his character than you would learn through dinner and a movie. Not only is this a casual and less stressful way to meet men, it's also getting you involved in the world around you. I highly recommend that you choose a volunteer effort that you would be interested in regardless of the men. Volunteer work is often tedious. If you're there just to meet men, you probably won't last long. But if you're there because you're behind the cause, you'll enjoy what you're doing and meeting men will naturally occur as part of the process.

PARTIES

Expense: Free or the cost of going dutch with a date for coffee and dessert.

Dupe Factor: You could be easily deceived in the beginning, but less with time.

Time: A few hours per week/month.

Stress: Can create high anxiety and apprehension.

Parties can create a difficult situation for the sincerely marriage-minded woman. There's usually a lot of ice-breaking anxiety involved unless you get a good introduction from the host. Then you also have constant concerns about the way you're dressed, your breath, your hair, and your clothing—all this before you even know if a man you have your eye on is available or even interested in you. On the other hand, parties that are more subdued and more focused on mingling can be a great way to meet men because you have an opportunity to actually converse.

FRIENDS OF FRIENDS

Expense: Depends on how the introduction is made.

Dupe Factor: You could be easily deceived in the beginning, but less with time.

Time: Depends on the how the introduction is made.

Stress: Can potentially create high anxiety and apprehension.

Newsflash: You and your friends don't always have the same tastes in men. Your friends don't *really* know what you like in men. That goes for your female friends as well as your male friends. There's no way to find that out faster than to have someone fix you up. A friend of mine once fixed me up and I wanted to slap him. It was a total mismatch! Friends tend to pair you with people they like *for* you. In other words, people they think you would like based on how they view you. That may not necessarily be accurate, particularly if this isn't a really close friend who knows your most intimate thoughts and feelings. However, being fixed up has highly variable outcomes.

THE AUNT SALLY INTRODUCTION

Expense: Depends on how the introduction is
made.
Dupe Factor: You could be easily deceived in the
beginning, but less with time.
Time: Depends on how the introduction is
made.
Stress: Can create high anxiety and apprehension.

Everyone knows an Aunt Sally type. She may not actually be your aunt. In fact, she's probably just a sweet little old lady next door, at work, or at your church. Never underestimate the hookup power of these women. Little old ladies seem to know everyone. As a result, they know a lot of eligible single men. When Aunt Sally tells you that you should meet her best friend's son, you shouldn't just write it off. She might be right.

CASUAL INTERSECTIONS

Expense: None.

Dupe Factor: You could be easily deceived in the beginning, but less with time.

Time: Depends on when, where, and how the intersection occurs.

Stress: Anxiety equivalent to asking for a date.

Of all the people in your entire city, and in the entire world for that matter, you crossed the path of one special man while in line at the deli or while walking your dog through your neighborhood. It's the stuff great love stories are made of, and it could happen to you. But there is a downside:

1. The fact that you have chemistry when you meet doesn't ensure true compatibility. Furthermore, just because you meet in a seemingly fateful or romantic way doesn't mean you're destined to get married and live happily ever after.
2. When you meet men this way, you're left to the old method of spending hours on the telephone in cordial interrogations.

3. You may have to resort to on-the-date learning, which is what you're trying to avoid the stress of having to do in the first place.

First-Date Essentials

When you've met a man through most of the methods just mentioned, especially on the Internet, through dating services, and personal ads, he's a total stranger to you. Whether he's the best friend of a best friend, you've talked with him for hours and hours on the phone, exchanged long e-mails, or read his profile and seen his video, you still don't actually know him. Therefore, you can't be too careful with the first date. Here are some suggestions for making the first date safe and comfortable for you as well as him.

DON'T ACCEPT AN INVITATION TO HIS PLACE AND DON'T INVITE HIM TO YOURS

You should never meet at his place the first time. You don't know this man and he doesn't know you. Meet at a busy public place, such as a restaurant or coffee bar, so that you're not put in a vulnerable position. As an extreme example of why you shouldn't go to the home of someone you hardly know, consider this: I know a guy who went to a woman's house for a first date and was soon called in for questioning by the police. It turned out she was a murder suspect, and they saw his car in her driveway and thought he might be involved too. You can't be too careful, can you?

ALWAYS LET SOMEONE KNOW WHERE YOU'RE GOING TO MEET

Always let a friend know where you're going, when, and how long you expect to be there. You may even have a friend call you on your cell phone or page you while you're out and have them expect you to call them back. You also can slip away to a phone and call a friend during a date. If no one is available to check in with, at the very least, leave a message on your own voice mail so there's some record of your whereabouts. Doing this also gives you a chance to take a break from the date to gather your thoughts.

GO DUTCH

Going dutch is the best rule for the first date. That way nobody can cast expectations on the other person. Neither person feels used or feels they owe the other person anything. It helps to keep motives pure.

MEET HIM THERE

Agree to meet each other at the place of the date. This is important for several reasons. First, it's a safety precaution for both people. Second, it also allows you some time to gather your thoughts before and after the date. On the other hand, if he picked you up (or you picked him up), you'd have to make conversation all the way there and back. This way, if the date doesn't work out, you can both easily go your separate ways.

LISTEN TO WHAT YOUR INSTINCTS ARE TELLING YOU

If you have a hunch that something just isn't right, it probably isn't. While you don't want to be paranoid or hypersensitive to everything on the first date, you should listen to what your basic instincts are telling you about a person. What's your gut feeling? That clear little voice inside is never wrong.

BE COURTEOUS EVEN IF YOU DON'T FEEL A LOVE CONNECTION

If there's no strong attraction, it will be clear to you pretty fast. Believe me, I've been on both sides of this situation enough times to know how it feels. It's important to be courteous and enjoy your date anyway. Try not to hurt his feelings, but don't lead him on either. Next time you talk, politely explain to him that you didn't feel the right kind of connection, but you wish him well.

WHOA, DOWN GIRL!

You're sitting at a table, hidden in the corner of a restaurant with your eyes on the door, and he comes in. He's wearing a brown leather jacket and jeans, just as he said he would. It's him! And he looks even better than he said. Now your heart is thumping. You were already crazy about him from the long phone conversations. During the date, things go really well. You already know each other pretty well from the phone, and both of you are physically attracted to each other. You're both consenting adults. Why not take it to the next level right now?

STOP. Remember, you're looking for Mr. Right, not Mr. Right Now! I can't overemphasize the fact that jumping into the sack is the fastest way *not* to get to know somebody for who he really is. Good sex is so intoxicating that it makes it really difficult to see a person clearly. If you start out with a sexual relationship from the beginning, you can easily find yourself liking the sex more than the man. And you can't build a marriage on that, or even a successful relationship for that matter.

YOU HAVE NO TIME FOR THE DISHONEST

When you meet a man for the first time, ask yourself if he was honest with you in his description of himself. Never mind a little stretching of the facts—a few more pounds than he said, a little shorter than he said. Don't we all do that? Look for outright lies. For example, say you met him online and he e-mailed you a picture of himself at the beach in a skintight Speedo, but looking at him you can clearly see that he couldn't even fit one leg into that bikini swimsuit today—that's blatantly dishonest. I'm not talking about making superficial judgments about people based strictly on their looks. My focus here is on honesty. This is about the hours you've spent talking on the phone or e-mailing someone only to find out he's not the person he led you to believe he was. Can you trust a person with your heart if you can't even trust him to be honest about himself?

KEEP IT SIMPLE

Keep things light, fun, and inexpensive. For example, a public park on a weekend afternoon is a great first date because it allows lots of time to talk and plenty of props, such as feeding pigeons, watching people on a lake, horseback riding, swings, or watching children play. If you have lunch or dinner, go to a place where you can maximize conversation. Right now, you need to be getting to know him. On first dates, avoid the dinner and a movie date. Movies don't allow time for personal interaction, and it can be a long dinner if you're out with someone you're not enjoying the evening with.

BE YOURSELF

Don't act like someone on *The Dating Game* by saying what you think the other person wants to hear. Just be yourself and have fun. If you're playing the role of someone else, you can't keep doing it forever. And if you're interested in making a love connection that leads to a marriage, being yourself is the best place to begin.

Things to Think About

1. What were you taught about how to meet the right man?
2. Have the traditional methods of meeting men worked for you?
3. Have you tried any innovative ways of meeting men? Why or why not?
4. What are some ways you can reduce the amount of stress, time, and frustration you experience in the dating world?
5. What experiences have you had with on-the-date learning?

Journal Exercise

Write a personal ad about yourself using one hundred words or less. After you've written your ad, write a fictitious ad from the perspective of the type of man you want to meet. What's he looking for and why?

Inside the Mind of a Bachelor, Part 7

I remember my first little spat with Nancy. I was over at her place and she asked me to go get the mail for her, so I did. I wasn't checking through her mail for anything . . . well, okay, I'm not going to lie. I sifted through it on my way back up the stairs to her apartment to see if I could find any envelopes that looked like they were cards or letters from out-of-town boyfriends. I didn't see anything like that, but guess what I did find? She had a membership to Love On-line, the computer dating club!

I couldn't believe it. I couldn't see why a woman as hot as Nancy would go online to find a date. I started thinking she had a second life I didn't know about or something. I mean, I know we're not married, but it was my under-standing that we had something special and exclusive, so I confronted her with it.

Instead of getting angry, she laughed at me. She said it wasn't about simply meeting men, it was about meeting the *right* men. She told me that joining that computer dating club was the best thing she'd ever done because it helped her sift through men better than she'd had luck doing on her own.

But I was kind of jealous. All she had to do was sit down at the computer and point and click on dudes and send them e-mail. She saw I wasn't amused, and she assured me that she hadn't been to the site since we started getting serious. She said she was probably still on the mailing list.

But I wasn't satisfied. I wanted to know if she'd met any-one, and she said, "Yes, a couple of really nice guys, one flake, and one total jerk." She'd even met one of the nice guys for coffee, but said there was no chemistry.

On my way home, I got to thinking. A brother's got to really come correct with a woman if he wants to keep her these days because she can go global on you right from her computer. She can be scoping out dudes all over the coun-try, all over the world, these days. She doesn't have to be limited to the guy next door or across town. Of course, that means unlimited opportunities for players, but it changes their game too because a woman with her head on straight can read between the lines and figure out what a player is up to without ever having to meet him. The game will never be the same.

8

How to Avoid Being Played by the Players

I never said sifting through the available men out there would be easy. It takes time and patience, and while you're sifting, I can guarantee you that you'll meet plenty of the game players. First you have to understand that the number of players and knuckleheads is naturally higher than that of available good men. That's just a fact. Accept it. You and I both know that if you just wanted a man, any man, you could have one tomorrow. The real issue is finding the kind of man you really want.

First, you'll need some tools for survival. You need to know Playerspeak, the language of players, their games, and how to counteract them in a way that preserves your dignity and safety. Following is a primer on Playerspeak.

PLAYERSPEAK

Playerspeak is totally different from any language of men, even the Tinspeak I explained in my book *Understanding the Tin Man*. Playerspeak is the ultimate double talk because players are always maneuvering to get you into bed or into their harem so they can have access to you at their convenience. Unlike other forms of manspeak, Playerspeak is intentionally deceptive. Here are some examples:

I'M READY TO SETTLE DOWN.

This means: *I think you're the kind of woman who'll only give it up if I give you the impression I want a relationship.*

Players aren't crazy. They know that games must be customized to the type of woman they're trying to play. If a player feels that a woman he's lusting after is the type of woman who'll sleep with him only if they're heading toward a commitment, he'll play right along and act as if he's seeking a relationship.

WE SHOULD MOVE IN AND GIVE IT A TRY.

This means: *It would be a lot more convenient for me if I had you under my thumb so you can't be with other men while I continue to play the field.*

Notice, he only wants to move in together, he doesn't want to be married. The gaming of some players isn't limited to bouncing from woman to woman with no strings attached. Some players want to have a woman who serves as their home base, so to speak. She's the one who gives him a feeling of stability. In essence, he's just playing house with her. Meanwhile, he doesn't curtail his bed hopping, he just goes underground with it. However, be aware that some players will take it a step further by actually marrying a woman in order to get a home base, while not really ever intending to be fully committed to the relationship.

I USED TO BE A PLAYER, BUT NOW I'M DIFFERENT.

This means one of two things:

1. *In my mind, I've changed, but I'm still a player at heart.*

This may sound crazy, but it's actually true. Some players decide they're going to change and reform from being players, and they even make a declaration to themselves or their friends about it. But that's where it ends. They say they've changed, but they don't follow their words with actions when their old habits prove difficult to break.

2. *I really have changed, but it's an ongoing struggle.*

This is a sort of confession. Unlike other Playerspeak, it's not intentionally deceptive. Men who've changed and are working hard not to be players again find it therapeutic to reaffirm this in the presence of a woman. It's the same as a recovering alcoholic openly admitting that he used to be an alcoholic.

It's important to realize that players *can* change their ways. But it's a difficult process that doesn't happen overnight. It's a deprogramming that a man has to undergo willingly and be serious about. He has to work at maintaining his new lifestyle because the lure of the game is always there.

I DON'T LIE ABOUT BEING A PLAYER. I JUST TELL WOMEN STRAIGHT UP WHAT I'M ALL ABOUT.

This means: *I tell women enough about me to make it seem as though I'm being open and honest about myself and my lifestyle. But it's all just part of my game.*

He's lying. Players don't ever come straight out with everything because the intent of a player is to maintain the upper hand. A woman may indeed know a lot about him. She may even know she's not his only woman. But she never really knows the true extent of his game because that is his secret game plan—it's the way he keeps the upper hand. If a woman were to know too much about his life, she could disempower his scheme, and he's not about to let that happen. Therefore, no matter how much of his history or how supposedly honest he is with you, the worst is omitted or glossed over, if mentioned at all.

I DON'T TRY TO PLAY WOMEN, THEY COME AFTER ME. WHAT AM I SUPPOSED TO DO, SAY I'M NOT INTERESTED?

This means: *As long as I'm getting what I want, I just let women think what they want to think about us having some kind of relationship.*

He has a point. As I mentioned earlier, as viewed from a man's perspective, the competition among women for eligible bachelors is fierce. Bachelors know this and use it as a competitive advantage. However, the player who makes such a statement is the type who won't do anything to discourage a woman who pursues him aggressively. Instead of saying he isn't interested, he simply adds the pursuing woman to his harem and strings her along.

I JUST GOT OUT OF A BAD RELATIONSHIP AND I'M NOT READY TO GET SERIOUS.

This means: *I had a bad experience in a relationship and I'm going to milk it for all it's worth.*

It seems every player is dragging around the ghosts of a bad relationship as an excuse for playing the field. It's that old girlfriend who hurt him so badly that he just can't see himself getting involved again. For some guys, there may be some truth to the too-hurt-to-jump-back-in attitude. In those cases, they should stay on the sidelines until they're emotionally capable of handling a relationship again. But it's different with players. Players aren't getting over a relationship anymore. They just feel it's a convenient excuse to explain their lifestyle, or they may even feel they can garner some sympathy using this line.

I'M OPEN TO GETTING INTO A RELATIONSHIP WITH THE RIGHT WOMAN.

This means: *I really would love to be in a relationship, but my urge to be a player is greater than my urge to have a relationship.*

This is a red flag because it uses an intentionally ambiguous definition. Players meet a lot of women. No doubt the average player wouldn't know if a good woman were standing right in front of him because he's too busy with his schemes. Therefore, for a player to say he's open to a relationship with the right woman is just his way of playing games with a woman because the door to his heart isn't open to forming a relationship in the first place.

GAMES OF PLAYERS

The next tool women need to avoid being played is to know more about the games of players. Following are some typical games. As you read, be mindful that I'm speaking specifically of players and their abuses of these situations. The following definitions don't apply to men who aren't players. Remember, players often use the same techniques as good men; the difference is more in the motive than in the actions.

For example, below I discuss the man who creates the

illusion that he just seems too good to be true. In contrast, some guys may actually be good men and seem too good to be true. That's why much of player identification comes down to being able to be your own best advisor. Becoming familiar with the typical head games of players is a great way to start. See Chapter 7, "How to Sift Through All the Game Players to Find Mr. Right," as well.

1. MASTER OF SMOOTH TALK

The Master of Smooth Talk isn't just another smooth talker, he's the best of the best. He's the man who can say just the right thing, in just the right way, to light a woman's fire. His game is to walk right up to a woman and to engage her in conversation. His conversations always flow flawlessly back and forth, like a rhythm. Talking with him is like listening to a song because it flows so smoothly.

2. THE ILLUSIONIST

This is the player who somehow seems to be interested in everything that interests you and seems to be everything you could want in a man in every possible way. He's a master of illusions. Like a magician, his specialty is to divert your attention from reality while he dazzles you with moves that are more sleight of hand than reality.

3. VERBAL BOUNDARY TESTER

In this game, the player speaks in a suggestive way to find out what boundaries a woman has. This is usually in the form of sexually suggestive remarks and innuendos. He will usually start with words or phrases that could have a double meaning. If that doesn't work, he'll make less subtle suggestions. If the woman plays along, he takes that as a green light for more of the same.

4. PHYSICAL BOUNDARY TESTER

The physical boundary tester often continues what the verbal boundary tester has begun. However, some players go directly to testing physical boundaries, skipping the verbal tests altogether. In this technique, a player uses a simple touch as a test of the woman's boundaries. If he likes the result of his test, he'll proceed to the next phase of this game. For example, while sitting and talking, he may simply touch her on the arm. After gauging her reaction, he'll try another touch, perhaps on her knee or thigh. If she responds favorably or even neutrally, he feels he is free to touch her.

5. COMER AND GOER

The comer and goer is easy to detect. In this game, the player makes himself available to a woman only when he wants to be available. This player doesn't seem to call often. He's always busy, unless he doesn't want to be. He's not dependable, and he tends to be inconsistent with his actions.

6. DRAMA KING

Some players use drama as a tool by which to create emotional ties to women. They go into jealous tirades, provoke highly emotionally charged conversations, or just plain do acting jobs to make it seem as if they are emotionally into a woman. However, they're really attempting to manipulate her.

7. DEPENDENCE CREATOR

The player using this technique is more sinister. In this scenario, the player attempts to get a woman dependent on him in any way he can: emotionally, physically, or even financially. After he succeeds in making her dependent on him, he can have the relationship take any form that best suits him because the woman is always motivated by the fear of losing him.

8. HAREM BUILDER

The harem builder is less playing a game and more exhibiting a basic element of his lifestyle. Players build harems. The strategy is always to have a woman available for their varying moods and desires. Therefore, a player's harem will have a wide range of women who are being constantly shuffled, promoted in their rankings, demoted, or dropped from the lineup. For more on this, refer back to Chapter 1, "Why Buy the Cow When You Can Get the Milk for Free?"

9. LONG-DISTANCE LOVER

Players love to be long-distance lovers, as this strategy allows them to have a number of benefits with minimal responsibilities. The long-distance player always can use distance as a reason to avoid a commitment, while still having someone who cares deeply for him. He also has the option to fly in for a hot weekend and then go back to his other women at home.

10. OLD FLAME SPARKER

Players who spark the old flame are preying on the emotional nature of women. It's a favorite old game. The old flame can get sparked in a couple of ways. In one scenario, a player may have fond memories of a woman from his past and decide to initiate contact with her. In another scenario, he may have a chance encounter with an old flame and find her attractive. The player who tries to spark an old flame attempts to revive old feelings and passions instantly for the purposes of a quick score. Afterward, he fades off quickly again. This game is especially prevalent around holidays.

11. MR. FRIENDLY

Mr. Friendly is the player who sets up his game by using a most subtle form of seduction. He plays the great guy role and waits patiently until it's time to strike. He comes off as a Mr. Nice Guy or a girl's best friend type, while not allowing himself to be categorized as a neutered nice guy type. Usually Mr. Friendly already has a harem. Therefore, he is free to develop a situation patiently so that when the right time comes, "something can just happen" (as the woman sees it). For him, it was strategy all along.

How to Turn a Player's Game on Him

So how do you win in the games these players are playing? Following are concrete strategies you can use to foil their plots and run off these Mr. Wrongs.

1. MASTER OF SMOOTH TALK

The mistake some women make with the Master of Smooth Talk is that they equate his smooth talk to his level of interest in them. Wrong! The Master of Smooth Talk is interested in testing himself, using you as the test. He's not as much interested in you as he is in seeing if he can get you.

To break up his game, you have to diffuse him. In essence, you've got to slow him down and put on the brakes. Move him out of his familiar territory, which is verbal seduction. Take the conversation into other areas and levels where he can't play his game of seduction, topics such as politics or education. More than likely, he won't have as much to say when you turn the conversation to things other than leisurely topics, because he doesn't have the capacity to discuss or even have much interest in things other than pursuits of pleasure.

2. THE ILLUSIONIST

When a player is attempting to make himself appear to be everything you could possibly want in a man, and more, it's time to throw him a curve ball. Instead of you doing all of the talking, get him to talk more. This won't be difficult because men love to talk about themselves. As he begins to talk, you will find out more about him through what he says than you will if you're doing all of the talking and he's simply agreeing with you. For an Illusionist to be successful, he needs information from you. If you make him divulge his information first, he loses that advantage.

3. VERBAL BOUNDARY TESTER

Unless you're open to a man's innuendos, you have to send him a message that you're not interested. To thwart this verbal game, a woman has to avoid giving mixed signals. Thinking you can laugh his verbal advances away isn't a good strategy. Instead, try giving him silence or a blank face when he makes unwanted innuendos. That should do the trick. But sometimes players are persistent. They'll repeat their remark, thinking you must not have heard it or that you'll soften up a little the second time around. That's when you may have to say something direct, such as "Let's steer this conversation in another direction."

4. PHYSICAL BOUNDARY TESTER

Unless you want a man to touch you, you should give a very direct negative response to his touch. This is one of those no-means-no situations. You'll have to tell him in no uncertain terms that he is not to touch you. Another approach is to shift abruptly and awkwardly as he attempts to touch you. But the best approach is to tell him not to touch you because you don't want to leave any room for misunderstanding.

5. COMER AND GOER

This one is easy. Just don't play the game with him. It takes two people to make the come-and-go game work. If you simply become unavailable to a man who is trying to play this game with you, either he'll have to start taking time with you more seriously or he'll move his game on to someone else.

6. DRAMA KING

When dealing with a Drama King, the best strategy is to not go there with him. When players attempt to use drama, they're assuming that the woman will revert to her emotional nature and become moved by his display of emotions. If you detect a player is attempting to manipulate your emotions, don't go there with him. If he's faking, he'll quickly see that he's running into a brick wall and he'll back off.

7. DEPENDENCE CREATOR

The way to avoid being caught in the snare of a player who wants you to be dependent on him is to keep things on an equal level. Regardless of who makes the most money, relationships can be balanced. Don't allow him to always pay for everything. Don't allow him to be your only friend, counselor, or confidant. Continue to keep your relationships with your friends alive. Have a life other than with this man. That way, your interaction with him is healthy, not needy.

8. HAREM BUILDER

Unknown to you, you're probably in some guy's harem. Whether you have a sexual relationship doesn't determine whether he considers you to be in his harem. To be honest, there's not much you can do about that unless you're in a relationship with him, in which case he shouldn't have a harem anymore!

You can't know everything, but you can set certain boundaries to make sure that the men with whom you interact respect you and treat you with dignity. That alone is the most important factor. You can't control whether he's trying to play the field because you may not always know it up front. But you can control how he treats you. Your best strategy here is to be yourself and not allow yourself to be manipulated. Insist on being respected and stand firm on your principles. If he doesn't appreciate those things, he'll do you both a favor by excusing himself from your life.

9. LONG-DISTANCE LOVER

The player who's attempting to be Romeo by remote is counting on distance to be the tool with which to play you. If you detect your long-distance man is attempting to play you, try calling his bluff. In other words, arrange to see each other more often for longer periods of time. This may be enough to show you his true colors. If that doesn't work, or if it is impractical, just don't get too serious too fast and allow time for the truth to emerge. Players can attempt to fool you for a little while, but eventually they fall back into their old habits and patterns again. Either way, if you don't rush things, the truth will become clear through the circumstances.

10. OLD FLAME SPARKER

When players are attempting to spark an old flame to have a quick romance, their strategy is to play on shared history. The first step is to avoid basing everything today on what happened yesterday. Second, look at the circumstances. Is he recently divorced, bored in a relationship, in town for a hot minute, or in any other type of situation in which a quick romance would be of benefit to him? That's the game with the old flame, to have a quick romance because all of the foundational work has been done already. This player wants to pick up where he left off when it's convenient to him.

11. MR. FRIENDLY

Mr. Friendly is a tough player to resist because he's so smooth. After all, he uses seemingly genuine friendship as the approach to endear himself to you; under the surface, however, he has a desire to take you to bed. Often you get a gut feeling about this guy that he isn't all he's saying he is. Though he seems to be harmlessly friendly, you sense he's not at all to be mistaken for a harmless nice guy type.

If you feel a player is trying to come into your life by posing as Mr. Friendly, your best bet is to keep things on the friendly level and not let them go any further. If he wants to be more than friends, he'll have to make his true intentions known openly instead of using his back-door approach.

Things to Think About

1. Which of the players from this chapter have you encountered? How did you handle your encounters with them?
2. Although you must be careful in the dating world, how can you avoid becoming pessimistic or overly critical of men you meet?
3. What do you think about the way players build harems? Do women do the same thing? What's the difference between building a harem and simply dating?

Journal Exercise

Finding out you've been played is a painful experience. It leaves you angry, distrustful of men, and often without closure to a relationship in which you've invested yourself wholly.

How did you put yourself back together and go on with your life? What are some constructive ways to get over being played by a player? Describe several things a woman can do to move on with her life and to heal from the pain, particularly when there was an abrupt ending with no closure. Describe how each of your suggestions would help a woman heal.

Inside the Mind of a Bachelor, Part 8

I've played the women. I can't believe some of the things I've gotten away with. But you can't play all women. Some women just can't be played. I remember a couple from my past who just didn't go there. One was this babe, Theresa, whom I wanted to get with since high school. Man, she wasn't down with anything sexual. She'd kiss like a maniac and neck, but that was it. I tried in high school and college and got nowhere. She probably got married as a virgin. I don't know where she got all of that willpower from. But I have to admit, I respect her for it because I threw my best at her.

And there was this other honey, Monica. She wouldn't even give me the time of day. She even told me straight up one day, "You're a player and I'm not into playing games."

Usually even when a babe says something like that, you still have a chance because they can't help but be attracted to that bad boy in you. But not Monica; she meant it and I could feel it. I could tell she meant it because she wasn't even rude, she just said it all matter-of-factly. I don't know how she read me like that. But she was right. I tried to talk to her a few more times. But eventually I just left her alone.

And then there's Nancy. She makes a brother respect her. With a honey like her you either have to come correct or get to steppin'. And it sounds crazy, but another thing I like about Nancy is that she can read players (because she read me) and I don't have to worry about her going out and getting smooth-talked by some Don Juan because she isn't easily fooled. Men want a woman who can't just be swept away by the first guy who comes along. I don't have to worry about that with Nancy.

9

What Single Women Have to Say About Bachelors Who Avoid or Resist Marriage and Commitment

For this book, I conducted a survey on the web, by e-mail, and at some of my events to get single women's candid statements about men who avoid or resist marriage and commitment. The women had plenty to say. In fact, men could learn a whole lot from these women who were very specific about their feelings.

As an added feature, this chapter is designed to be interactive. After each issue, you're invited to complete a journal entry. Try a few of them, or do them all. Even if you don't have direct experience with some of the issues in this chapter, you still can write responses to the issues. The journaling may help make the issues more relevant to your life and experiences. The following statements were collected from the responses of single women of various ages from all over the United States, with some from Canada and even a few from England. What struck me as fascinating was the universality of the concerns these women had. It didn't seem to matter what age, ethnicity, or part of the world they were from; women seemed to have basically the same issues with bachelors.

BACHELORS ARE AFRAID OF RESPONSIBILITY.

Men who run [from commitments] are scared. They don't want the responsibility and the give and take of love. They just want to take!

—*Ella, 27*

Journal Exercise
What has your experience been with dating selfish or egotistical men? If you've ever dated such men, where and how did you draw the line with them?

MOST SINGLE MEN CAN'T HANDLE A RELATIONSHIP WITH A REAL WOMAN.

Men run from women who have all the qualities they say they want. They're really afraid of the kind of women they say they want.

—*Andrea, 37*

Journal Exercise

Do you feel that you've been exactly what a man said he wanted, but he still didn't want to commit? What was the problem? Do you feel that men don't really know what they want? Do you think he simply wasn't being honest about what he really wanted? Or do you think some women try too hard to tell men what they want or need in a relationship?

MEN DON'T WANT TO GROW UP.

The men I meet are just like the boys I dated in college.
All they talk about is sex and their cars.

—Terry, 23

Journal Exercise

In your experience with single men, have you found them to be overly interested in cars, sports, and making money? At what point do you feel a relationship begins to take on importance to a man? Why?

BACHELORS HAVE TOO MANY WOMEN CHASING AFTER THEM.

They [men] have so many women to choose from that
they feel they can get away with anything.

—Kathy, 30

Journal Exercise

Do you feel that the number of available women makes men more apt to play the field? Do you think this is something men are doing consciously, or would they be the same regardless of the numbers? How do some women allow men to feel they can get away with anything?

A GUY IS RULED BY THE HEAD IN HIS PANTS.

I don't care what they say, they all just want to get laid.

—*Chrissy, 27*

Journal Exercise

Do men always see sex as a top priority with women, or does this attitude have more to do with the stage of bachelorhood a man is in? Have you ever felt hurt or betrayed by finding out a man you thought highly of was actually just trying to get you into bed? How did you heal from the pain?

SOME MEN WANT WOMEN TO TAKE CARE OF THEM.

I think men like being taken care of. They want a wife for doing the laundry and cooking, and for the free sex, back scratches, and soup in bed when they are sick.

They also want a wife to bring in additional, or all of, the income.

—Amy, 34

Journal Exercise

Name three signs that might signal to a woman that a man she's involved with may want her to take care of him in some way. Where's the fine line between a woman taking care of a man and her being a faithful mate?

MEN ARE LOOKING FOR SOMETHING UNREAL IN A WOMAN.

They don't want to get married, saying they can't find the right woman. But it's because they want a woman who is perfect in every way. If the slightest thing is out of place, they don't want to give a girl the time of day.

—Alexis, 29

Journal Entry

What pressures do women today feel to be perfect? Do you feel the romantic market requires that you have to measure yourself against superwoman standards?

DON'T LET ONE BAD RELATIONSHIP RUIN YOU FOR LIFE.

Once a man has had one bad relationship, he'll use that as an old tired excuse to avoid commitment the rest of his life.

—*Gina, 44*

Journal Exercise

How many times do you recall a man using a past hurt as a reason to not get into a relationship? Was the result a friendship or did you go your separate ways? Or did you get involved with him anyway? If so, what happened?

STOP HOLDING YOUR PRESENT WOMAN RESPONSIBLE FOR A WOMAN IN YOUR PAST.

I am sick and tired of men wanting me to feel bad for what other women did to them in the past. When it's the other way around, they always tell us it wasn't them who hurt us in the past. Why can't they apply that to thinking to themselves?

—*Dianna, 28*

Journal Exercise

Are women more emotionally resilient than men? Why does it seem women will recover from a hurtful relationship and give another relationship a chance whereas men seem to take longer and carry grudges after being hurt?

DON'T BE TOO BUSY WITH OTHER THINGS TO FOCUS ON RELATIONSHIP.

While you're trying to conquer the world, take some time out for love.

—Helen, 31

Journal Exercise

Have you ever felt a man loved you, but at the same time you felt you were only the second or third priority in his life? How did you resolve the situation with him?

ALL WOMEN AREN'T THE SAME.

Treat us as unique individuals, not as women as a group.

—Eboni, 22

Journal Exercise

What factors in society contribute to men initially seeing all women as having the same characteristics instead of seeing them as individuals?

NICE GUYS DON'T FINISH LAST; IT DEPENDS ON THE WOMAN.

Nice guys don't finish last. It all depends on what type of woman is judging the race.

—*Angie, 35*

Journal Exercise

Why do you think nice guys feel slighted in the dating game? Is it a myth that women like bad boys more than nice guys? What do some women find exciting about bad boys? Is preference for bad boys a stage some women go through?

DON'T BELIEVE THAT ALL WOMEN WANT TO TRAP YOU.

I have my own career, a nine-year-old daughter, a house, a dog, and a cat. I'm also a good woman with a lot to offer as a wife and lover. I do want a man in my life, but I'm not out to trap a man to get him into my life.

—*Jeanette, 36*

Journal Exercise

What makes men feel that women are out to trap them into commitment or marriages? Can you identify anything you've said or done that would make a man feel he's being trapped? Has a man ever told you that he felt you were attempting to trap him into a relationship?

REALIZE WHAT YOU HAVE.

Stop leaving only to come back after realizing how well you had it in the first place.

—*Leeann, 19*

Journal Exercise

Can you recall a time (or times) when a man has left your life, only to return desiring to rekindle the romance? Did you give him a second chance? If so, what was your motivation: fear of losing him or a belief it could work? What happened as a result of your decision?

MAKE YOUR TRUE INTENTIONS KNOWN UP FRONT.

Stop playing so many games . . . it's easier on both of us in the long run.

—*Candace, 24*

Journal Exercise

Why do you feel some men think it's necessary to play games even after you've asked them to be honest and up front with you? Name three potential warning signs that a man may be a game player.

WOMEN WANT TO FEEL LOVED AND DESIRED.

Women need to feel special and loved. We also want to feel like our man desires and loves us more than anyone in their past. That is one thing men need to remember.

—*Lonnie, 37*

Journal Exercise
Have you ever been in a relationship in which you felt the ghost of another woman was always present and creating problems in your relationship? When did you realize he was still mentally involved with his ex? What is the best way to handle such a situation?

REALIZE THAT OUR THOUGHTS COME FROM HOW WE FEEL.

Our thoughts are anchored in what we feel often intuitively and without logical explanation! If what we think and feel conflict, we often tend to lead with our emotions, our spiritual antenna, because we trust that more than the cold facts.

—*Rochelle, 26*

Journal Exercise

Why do men and women often see the same situation differently? Is it a case of one being wrong and the other being right, or are there just natural differences? How can a couple work together to communicate effectively despite their differences?

UNDERSTAND THAT A WOMAN CAN COMPLEMENT AND BALANCE YOU.

> *Learn to embrace a woman's qualities . . . instead of being frustrated and resentful of how a woman is wired, embrace it!*
>
> —*Michelle, 34*

Journal Exercise

This entry can be a follow-up to the previous journal entry. Write about how it makes you feel when a man summarily dismisses your opinion simply because you're a woman. Have you ever been involved with a man whom you found to be misogynistic?

10

Questions and Answers About Bachelors

I receive lots of e-mail from women with various questions about men and relationships. The following questions and answers are typical of many of the topics on which I've been asked to comment about bachelors. This chapter is interactive. For each question, there's opportunity for a short journal response in which you can add your feelings on the issue. Also, you can go to my website, www.williamjuly.com, and participate in the online discussion of these issues.

1. WHY DO SOME MEN PURSUE RELATIONSHIPS WITH HOOCHIE-MOMMA TYPES AND PASS RIGHT BY THE GOOD WOMEN?

Answer: For many men, a high-heeled, fast woman in a tight short skirt seems to be a dream come true. With this woman, the hoochie-momma, some men are deluded into seeing what they believe is a dream girl. She's sexy and she requires no real commitment or true responsibility. Men usually treat hoochie-mommas well, giving them gifts and money. It seems that all is well, but it isn't. It's an inherently unstable relationship. He only treats her well as long as she doesn't become a nuisance to him. If she starts to have too many problems for him to deal with, or if she dares to push for some sort of relationship that isn't convenient to him, he'll leave her in an instant.

Ultimately, the cost of such a relationship to a man can be large. For one thing, he's depriving himself of intimacy, which as a human being he has a natural craving for. His arrangement with his hoochie-momma can't provide that. Second, the long-term cost of this type of relationship is that he will become emotionally numb and it will become increasingly difficult to connect with women emotionally. If he continues these sexual quid pro quo arrangements, one day he'll find himself wanting a real relationship but having extreme difficulty sustaining it because he won't know how to embrace real intimacy.

Journal Exercise

What motivates some women to be hoochie-mommas? What defines a hoochie-momma, her clothing or her attitude?

2. HOW DO I KNOW IF A GUY IS SERIOUS OR JUST A PLAYER PLAYING GAMES?

Answer: Like so many of these questions, there's no simple answer. First, examine how you feel. Do you feel something isn't right? That's your first sign. If you're constantly feeling uncomfortable about this man, you should go with your instincts. Second, do you see red flags popping up? Things such as getting caught in lies, only being interested in sex, or being available only at specific times of the day and week are red flags to look out for.

Any woman, no matter how careful, can be caught in player's trap. But it shouldn't keep happening over and over. Some of the women who get caught by a player seem to be attracted only to men who fit the playboy profile. They shouldn't be the ones complaining. But as for the women who try to avoid them but seem to meet them anyway, I say be careful but also be balanced. Don't be so busy being Sherlock Holmes that you can't ever enjoy a date. Watch for signs and trust your instincts. And when in doubt, err on the side of caution.

Journal Exercise

Have your initial gut feelings about a man ever proven to be true? What red flags have you seen in the past that you ignored? What happened as a result of ignoring those caution signs?

3. WE'VE BEEN DATING FOR WHAT SEEMS LIKE FOREVER, BUT HE DOESN'T ACKNOWLEDGE ME AS HIS GIRLFRIEND. WHAT AM I TO HIM?

Answer: It depends. There are so many definitions and understandings of what "boyfriend" and "girlfriend" mean today. To me, it means an exclusive relationship. If he's not even willing to acknowledge you as his girlfriend, then you already know the score. Don't sit there trying to read anything into it; he's telling you with his actions that he doesn't consider himself to be in a relationship with you. Sure, he wants all of the benefits, but he wants to duck the responsibilities. As long as you play along, he will continue to avoid the commitment. Tell him to get in or out of the water, and be prepared to stick to the ultimatum if he balks.

Journal Exercise

How long should it take for a man to know if he wants to commit to a woman? Why?

4. I'M TIRED OF MEN SAYING THEY AREN'T READY FOR A RELATIONSHIP. WHEN IS A MAN EVER READY FOR A RELATIONSHIP?

Answer: Great question. He's ready when *he's* ready. Not when you're ready for him to be ready. Not when he's a certain age. Not when society's traditions say it is time. A man could have some logical reasons for not being ready, and he could have some seemingly illogical reasons. But the fact of the matter is that regardless of whether it's fear, playing the field, or whatever, he's not ready. If he feels he's not capable of handling a relationship, that's answer enough. And if you're interested in a relationship, he's not the right man. Some men may never be ready. Others eventually will grow into a mindset of wanting a loving and intimate relationship.

Journal Exercise

Reflect on dating a man who was reluctant to commit, or on a past relationship with a reluctant man. Did you try to make him want to commit? If so, why did you feel compelled to make him commit? What was the result of your efforts?

5. HE SAYS HE CAN'T HANDLE A RELATIONSHIP. WHAT DOES HE MEAN BY THAT?

Answer: He's probably referring to all of the things he perceives will be required of him in a relationship. He's thinking in terms of the total package. First, there's the emotional sum of things. We all know what an emotional roller coaster a relationship can be, even a good one. In saying he can't handle a relationship, he may be stating honestly that he's not in a place where he can handle the moods, thoughts, feelings, and time commitment required in a relationship.

Another thing he could be referring to is the financial commitment required in a relationship. When men think about relationships, we don't just think of the feelings and closeness. We think of money. One of our first thoughts when we think of being in a relationship is "Can I afford to be in a relationship with this woman?" It's just a reality for us. Is she high maintenance or low maintenance? And realistically, even the most low-maintenance relationship will require money for dates, gifts, and entertainment. That's an important consideration to men. If he feels he's not able to treat a woman they way he feels she deserves to be treated, he probably will resist getting too deeply involved.

Journal Exercise

How important is timing when it comes to meeting the right man? Have you ever met the right man but at the wrong time (for either him or you)?

6. I GET SO TIRED OF HEARING SUCCESSFUL ELIGIBLE BACHELORS SAY THEY AREN'T MARRIED BECAUSE THEY HAVEN'T MET THE RIGHT WOMAN YET. THERE ARE SO MANY GOOD WOMEN

OUT THERE, HOW CAN THEY SAY THEY HAVEN'T MET THE RIGHT ONE YET?
Answer: Three reasons:

1. Simply stated, many successful bachelors are having so much fun with such a broad choice of eligible women that they don't want to choose just one. They play the field and enjoy relationships with several women until they decide they want to have a wife and kids, then they pick one.
2. Some guys actually are afraid to settle down because they think that the minute they do, they're going to meet someone with a better body, a prettier face, and a more impressive résumé. Such men will never be satisfied.
3. Then there's the man who thinks that when he meets the right woman, everything will just happen perfectly and with magical flair. Unfortunately, this is a complete fantasy, and there is no way reality will match it.

Just because a man doesn't want to get married doesn't mean there's something wrong with him. There's no rule in life that says everyone has to get married. That's each individual's choice, and we must all respect that. A healthy decision not to marry is better than bending to social pressure to marry and being unhappy, having affairs, and hurting his loved ones and himself.

Journal Exercise

What pressures do you think men have about getting married? How do you feel men respond to pressures to get married?

7. IT SEEMS EVERY MAN I MEET IS A TIN MAN (I.E., A MAN WHO AVOIDS INTIMACY). WHY DO I KEEP MEETING THESE GUYS?

Answer: On one hand, I think it's probability. When women say they can't meet the right person, I think one part of it is in the numbers. The guys out there who are real jerks are usually much bolder and more aggressive about meeting women. That's because they have a scheme working. They are looking for the next unsuspecting woman they can use for their own ends.

On the other hand, the good men don't have time or energy to be out chasing women constantly. Also, many of them have grown shy of cold approaches in public because rejection can be so painful and embarrassing. That's not to say that no good men make cold approaches, because they do. They are just less inclined to do it. Last, I think you have to look within yourself. If you keep meeting the same jerks, there is quite possibly some pattern about the way you meet men that you need to take a close look at. Get creative, try personal ads, the Internet, and dating services. Take charge of the process instead of expecting Mr. Right to walk up and say "Hello."

Journal Exercise

Do you meet the types of men you feel compatible with? Why or why not? If you don't meet many men you feel compatible with, name three things you can do to change that situation.

8. WILL A MAN LOVE ME MORE IF I GIVE HIM SEX?

Answer: No, but he may lust after you more. Any woman who thinks the way to a man's heart is under the sheets is fooling herself. A relationship, whether short or long term, that is based on sex doesn't have much of a foundation. It won't take long for it to be tested, and it is likely to crumble. What often happens is people start enjoying sex but don't even know each other. Then as they get to know each other, they sometimes find out they don't really like the person as much as the sex. Still, they stick around because they're used to the good sex until, finally, things in the bedroom aren't worth the drama outside the bedroom.

Again, the answer is no. Sex may get him to love having sex with you and it may get you more attention and time with a man, but he won't necessarily love you.

Journal Exercise

What role should sex play in dating? Do you feel couples should avoid sex before a commitment or marriage? Why or why not?

9. WHAT DO MEN WANT FROM WOMEN IN BED?

Answer: Speaking in general terms, I believe men want excitement and variety in bed. Of course, a person's sexual desires can be as varied as the types of different personalities on the face of the earth. What's important is that there be two consenting adults involved who respect and honor each other. They will only do things that are safe and mutually satisfying.

When it comes to what a woman can do to enhance her bedroom appeal, I think she should flip the script and look outside the bedroom. Lots of women can wear sexy lingerie and play seductress, so you have to go beyond that level to really keep a man interested. I think the woman who really knows how to please a man in bed starts outside the bedroom. Realistically, in the long run, sex is about more than bodies. You're not going to keep or lose a man who really loves you based on what happens in the bedroom. The bedroom is just going to be a reflection of other things going on in your life together. Take care of that and the rest will come together. It may still take some—for lack of a better word—practice. But that will be the fun part.

Journal Exercise
Reflect on the statement "Sex starts in the head, not in the bed." What does this mean in terms of a relationship?

10. SHOULD WOMEN BE LESS ASSERTIVE OR GO AFTER A MAN?

Answer: My advice is, if you see something you like, go for it! Life is too short to wait around for the right person simply to happen to approach you. If you see a man and you get the right vibes, take a chance. I'm not saying you should jump into bed with him or run straight to the altar. But it doesn't hurt to introduce yourself and take it from there.

Journal Exercise

Have you ever been in a situation in which a man caught your eye, perhaps you even exchanged warm glances, but he never made a move so you didn't get to meet him? If you have a similar opportunity in the future, what could you do to casually introduce yourself?

11. CAN I BE TOO AGGRESSIVE FOR A MAN?

Answer: The very idea that a woman can be too aggressive in her approach comes from the outdated belief that the man should always make the first move. I don't agree that the man should always make the first move; therefore, I don't really believe that a woman is being too aggressive simply by making her interest in a man known.

However, having said that, I'll add that all men want to feel some degree of leadership in the courting phase of a relationship. Therefore, some men may be taken aback by a forward woman. There's an art to being forward with men.

It requires that a woman be assertive enough to make her interest known, but then back off enough to let him lead, or at least feel that he's leading. Most men don't really lead in a courtship, they just think they do!

Journal Exercise

What have your experiences been with being assertive in introducing yourself to men or asking them out on dates?

12. WHAT MAKES A MAN DECIDE A WOMAN IS THE TYPE HE WILL USE?

Answer: Generally women who are emotionally needy or who give off signs of being desperate to have a man they can cling to are good candidates for being dogged. That's because they're willing to accept any type of treatment to have just about any kind of man in their lives. Men can read this clearly, particularly men who are controlling or manipulative, because they look for such women.

Journal Exercise

A man can try to use you, but you don't have to take it. Reflect on a time you felt a man was attempting to use you. What did you do? What did you learn from the situation?

13. WHAT DEFINES A GIRL YOU CAN TAKE HOME TO MOM?

Answer: A girl a man can take home to Mom is a woman who meets all of the requirements that he feels would make a good wife. However, depending on what stage of bachelorhood a man is in, he may not necessarily value these characteristics. A man in the discovery stage of bachelorhood may see the value of a girl he can take home to Mom, but he won't want her at the moment. He'll want to store her away for future use until he's finished his years of chasing women to take home to bed. On the other hand, a man transitioning out of bachelorhood is ready for such a woman and sees her as invaluable.

Journal Exercise

Do you think you're the kind of woman a man feels he can take home to Mom? If so, how has this benefited you at times and not benefited you at other times? If your answer was no, why do you feel a man wouldn't consider you the type he'd take home to Mom? How do you feel about that?

14. WHAT DO BACHELORS THINK ABOUT SPIRITUALITY?

Answer: This is a dividing line for bachelors, just as it is for other groups in our society. Some bachelors are very spiritual. They actively practice a religion or live by a set of spiritual principles. Others may see spirituality and religion as an abstraction. Still others may be outright hedonists. You should ascertain which type you're dealing with from the very beginning because spiritual values form the core of a person, and your spiritual beliefs must match in order for a long-term relationship to work. That's not to say you have to be the same denomination, religion, or have exactly the same beliefs. However, at the very least, your most basic spiritual principles should match.

Journal Exercise

What are your spiritual or religious values? How have your spiritual or religious beliefs affected your current relationship or dating/relationships in the past?

15. WHAT QUALITY IS MORE IMPORTANT TO A MAN SEEKING A WIFE, BEAUTY OR BRAINS?

Answer: Every man wants a woman who has the body of a centerfold, the looks of a supermodel, the heart of Mother Teresa, and the sexual skills of a porn star. But since that's not going to happen, he ultimately looks for a woman who meets his own criteria. There's not a single set of criteria because it depends on the man and his mind-set. Some men seek beauty first because they want a trophy wife. Others seek brains and stability first because they want a woman who is truly capable of being of mutual benefit in a long-term relationship. Realistically, there are a lot of women with both beauty and brains out there, and some men look for both.

Journal Exercise

What are the strongest attributes you'd bring into a marriage? What weaknesses do you have that could present a challenge in a marriage?

16. WHAT DO MEN FEAR MOST ABOUT MARRIAGE?

Answer: Basically, men fear that marriage will result in the loss of their freedom and individuality. They fear that marriage is the end of fun and the beginning of life tied down to a heavy mortgage, excessive bills, and a job they don't particularly like but need.

Journal Exercise

How do you feel about men's fears of losing their sense of self in a marriage? Are these fears shared by women as well?

17. IS IT TRUE THAT SUCCESSFUL MEN GET MARRIED FOR STATUS, NOT LOVE?

Answer: This isn't the case with every single successful bachelor who gets married. But there is certainly some truth to this theory in some instances. Right or wrong, marriage is seen in our society as a sign of maturity, a signal that a man has graduated to the next level. Therefore, some successful bachelors come to a point at which they feel their professional lives would benefit by their being married, and they marry more with the status of their bride in mind rather than the love they feel in their hearts.

Journal Exercise

Have you ever felt that a man you were involved with or dating was with you for your social status or social connections? If so, was it flattering or insulting? How did the situation resolve itself?

18. AREN'T DIVORCED MEN BETTER POTENTIAL HUSBANDS BECAUSE THEY'VE BEEN BROKEN IN?

Answer: Not necessarily. When it comes to divorced men, the question is, are they broken in or broken? Some men have been broken in by divorce and therefore know what they really want from their next relationship. They also have experience coexisting in a household with a wife. On the other hand, some men have been so embittered by divorce that they are too difficult to get along with in a relationship.

Journal Exercise

What emotional baggage do men carry after a divorce? What is a good length of time for a divorced man to wait before getting into a serious relationship? Have you ever been someone's rebound woman? What was that experience like?

19. I GAVE HIM AN ULTIMATUM: MARRIAGE OR BREAK UP. WHAT DO YOU THINK?

Answer: I never recommend giving a man an ultimatum when it comes to marriage because he may make the decision to get married just to keep you, even though he may not really desire to be married. This will only cause big problems later.

On the other hand, it's always appropriate to state your

position on marriage or commitment firmly. This is different from an ultimatum because you're not telling him he'd better do this or else. Sometimes men need a reality check to understand what they have, and there's no better creation on earth to do that than a woman. Women naturally play the role of conscience for men, reminding us of things that we try to avoid or forget.

Journal Exercise

If you've ever given a man an ultimatum about getting married or committing, reflect on the feelings that compelled you to give him an ultimatum. What was the result? What emotions were you feeling at that time? What's the difference between an ultimatum and simply stating the facts as you see them?

20. HOW CAN A WOMAN IDENTIFY AN ABUSIVE MAN?

Answer: Abusive or violent men usually wave big red flags early in a relationship. Though they may begin as some of the most charming men you'll ever meet, they will soon start losing their tempers, having outbursts, or demonstrating possessive behavior in a way that signals you to run. Beware; the facts on abusive men clearly show that it doesn't get any better, only worse, much worse.

Journal Exercise

Have you ever discovered that a man you were dating or involved with was abusive, violent, or had a history of being abusive? What did you do? How can women draw healthy boundaries for themselves to preempt becoming snarled in such relationships?

21. DO KIDS SCARE MEN OFF?

Answer: Yes and no.

Yes, they can scare men off if they're running around wild and undisciplined, or if they're older and always getting into trouble. Then sometimes it's not the children but their father (your ex) that the man doesn't want to have to deal with constantly.

On the other hand, kids don't scare off men who have time to become acquainted with them and the situation. Doing this allows men to develop a relationship with the kids, rather than feeling that they just come with the woman as a package. After a man forms a relationship with a woman's children, he's much more inclined to accept the responsibility of the children without remorse. Note: I don't suggest introducing men to your children until you have a serious relationship with them. Your children don't need to meet and spend time with every man you date. It's too confusing to them.

Journal Exercise

If you have children, how has this affected the way men respond to the idea of forming a commitment with you?

22. I CAN'T HAVE CHILDREN.
DOES THAT RUIN MY CHANCES OF
GETTING A GOOD MAN?

Answer: It doesn't ruin your chances of getting a good man, but you may have to be more selective because some men see marriage and having their own biological offspring as a combined goal. Therefore, you should make every effort to be involved with a man who either already has children and doesn't want any more, or is open to adoption or other methods of becoming a father, such as surrogate motherhood or foster parenting.

Journal Exercise

Why do you feel it is important to some men to have biological offspring? What factors do you think would contribute to a man embracing the idea of adoption, surrogacy, or foster parenting in lieu of having biological children?

23. CAN BACHELORS AND SINGLE
WOMEN BE PLATONIC FRIENDS?

Answer: First, let's look at the term "friends." Friends can mean a whole range of things depending on which bachelor you ask. But when we say platonic friends, we've specified that we're talking about a nonromantic interest. This gets complicated because some men are friends only with women they're interested in. Other guys are friendly but have romantic designs on a woman that they simply haven't acted on. To be quite honest, most bachelors don't have many women they see purely as platonic friends, with the exception of the occasional gal pal—who's seen as just one of the guys. Sure, there are lots of bachelors who have platonic friendships with women, but in reality, there's often the possibility of a little more than just friendship operating just below the surface in their minds.

Journal Exercise

Are you platonic friends with any bachelors? Do you ever feel a tinge of romantic possibility with any of them? What factors contribute to your feelings about platonic friendship being easier with some men rather than others?

11

How Does Rod's Story End?

By now you've become familiar with the workings of the mind of a bachelor at large through the monologues of Rod. But how does his story end? Is he transformed by a new awareness through his relationship with Nancy, or does he choose to continue living as what he terms "a confirmed bachelor"? How does Rod's story end? Based on what you know about Rod (and bachelors in general), choose your own ending for his story. In your opinion, which one is the most realistic ending for Rod?

A. He Runs Scared

After three months of being together, I told Nancy that I needed some time to think about where things were going. Only I didn't come right out and say it until she made me. I just started acting funny, you know, distant and aloof. But Nancy confronted me and wanted some answers about my change in behavior over the past couple of weeks. That's when I started talking. I was saying stuff that I didn't even know I was thinking. I told her it wasn't another woman. It wasn't anything that she said or did. I told her that to be honest about it, I was just afraid. Then after I said that, I got all choked up. I almost started crying when I told Nancy that I loved her and wanted to be with her the rest of my life. I stopped short of asking her to marry me. It was crazy. I had more emotions running through me than a woman with PMS.

I do love Nancy. But I just don't think I can do all of that commitment stuff. I mean, what if I try and fail miserably? Then we'll have to break up and we'll both be hurt and angry. It just seems like life is easier when you keep relationships at a nice safe level and don't let them get too deep.

B. Happily Ever After

I may sound like some corny guy in a movie, but I don't care. Nancy is the best woman ever to step into my life. She's everything I could want in a woman. I didn't say she was perfect, nobody is. But she's everything I could ever want. We've been together three months and I feel that it's been three years. Our souls are so familiar to one another that I feel we're connected on a higher level.

I can really see myself having a future with Nancy. Not because it feels like a fantasy, but because day-to-day reality with her is great. We've had our spats and arguments, but we've made up and not held a grudge. That's new to me in a relationship. She said it was new to her too. Like I said before, she's really cool. This is the kind of woman I can see myself having a life with. If things continue the way they're going, I'm going to ask her to marry me. That's right. I said I'm going to ask her to marry me. But I'm going to wait at least six more months. I want to make sure that we're not just overwhelmed and infatuated. I know that's not the case. But I love her so much that I want both of us to be 100 percent sure when I pop the question.

And when we get engaged, it's not going to be one of those frozen engagements that lasts for years. We're going to set a date and do it. All I can tell you is to look out for an invitation in the mail from me in the near future.

C. The Backslider

I'd just walked in the door from an early dinner with Nancy. The perfume from her hug was in my mustache and my leather jacket. I loved it when that happened. After three months of being in love with her, I still felt like a goo-goo-eyed schoolboy with a crush.

I was changing into a T-shirt and some shorts when the phone rang in the living room. I thought it might have been Nancy calling from her cell phone, so I ran to the caller ID in my blue briefs. But it wasn't Nancy. The caller ID read "Yvette Harris" and displayed a number I hadn't seen in two months. It was Yvette, the girl from the wedding with whom I'd had a quickie torrid affair. She must have been ready for another round. My first thought was just let the phone ring over to the call notes, then I wouldn't have to talk to her. She'd get the message if I didn't call her back. But with two more rings left before the phone switched over, I couldn't help myself. I picked it up.

I won't even go into the details because I'm not proud of myself for doing what I did. To make a long story short, I was right. She did want another round. She was talking in a seductive voice. She told me she'd been dating a guy since the time we had our encounter and they'd become serious, but broken it off. She was very frank and told me it had been weeks since she'd had a man and even longer since she'd really had a good session in the sack because the ol' boy didn't have much stroke. I told her I was involved and she said she didn't care because she just wanted a little of my time. I remember her saying in a sultry tone, "When we finish our little thing you can go right back to your girl-friend. I understand that you have business to handle." She was talking that old familiar language that I used to know so well and enjoyed so much. It hit something deep inside me. Something I thought was dead, but wasn't. To make a long story short, I went over to Yvette's place just before 11 P.M. and left a little after 2 A.M.

I'm not going to tell Nancy. I don't plan to lose our relationship over this. I just hope it doesn't happen again. But I can't guarantee that it won't. The mind is willing, but the flesh is weak.

D. Nancy Drops Him

I'd been with Nancy for three months, but it seemed like longer because we were always together. And when we weren't together, we talked for hours on the phone. I loved her and she loved me.

Nancy and I had already discussed and agreed to the fact that we were an official couple. The tags of "girlfriend" and "boyfriend" were mutually ours, and we had no problem with that. That's the way we saw each other and that's how I introduced her to my family, friends, and coworkers, and vice versa.

All was well until the night one of Nancy's girlfriends had a party. About 11:30, her girlfriend came running out of the kitchen with tears of joy in her eyes because her boyfriend had just proposed to her on one knee. Everything was cool. We toasted them and everybody was happy.

But then Nancy's friend, Lisa, looked at us and jokingly asked, "Have you two thought about getting hitched?"

Nancy smiled.

I displayed a blank face and Nancy took notice.

On the way home we had the worst argument we'd ever had. It went a little something like this:

We were driving along the freeway and neither of us

was saying anything. I could tell she was steaming about something. I went over things in my head that she could possibly be angry about from the evening. The answer kept coming back to the fact that I didn't make an affirmative comment when Lisa jokingly asked if we'd considered marriage.

Nancy finally broke the silence. "So do you see a future for us?"

"What do you mean?" I said. This is a standard passive defense men use when we need to scramble for some time to get our thoughts together when confronted.

"When Lisa made the joke about us getting married. You couldn't even bear to laugh about it. You looked as though you'd seen a ghost," she said.

"No, I didn't," I said. Denial is another tool men use to dodge the hot seat.

"I should've known you hadn't changed from your days as a player. Once a player, always a player. I guess you want me to just be your girlfriend for life so you can have all the conveniences without the commitment. That's how guys are. Why buy the cow when you can get the milk for free, right?"

"Well, we don't want to move too fast, baby," I answered.

"I didn't say we had to get married tomorrow, Rod. But now that the subject has come up, I am curious as to why you're so freaked about the idea," she said.

"I'm not saying that I'm not looking down the road to us being a lot more, but I just like to take my time," I answered.

"Except when it comes to sex, right?" I pulled in front of her apartment and she opened the car door. "You're missing the point. I'll say it once more and maybe this time it will penetrate your male ego. The point is, I'm not asking you to marry me tomorrow. But I don't want to be dating for the rest of my life either. I don't think we're on the same page. I fear I've made an error in judgment about you."

That was the last thing Nancy said before slamming my car door so hard that it rocked the car.

Every couple comes to a point at which they need to go to the next level, or go their separate ways. Nancy and I were there. No longer simply boyfriend and girlfriend, it was time to decide whether we were boyfriend and girlfriend heading toward an engagement.

Obviously we were seeing things differently. Sure, I was enjoying being with her—and she was the only woman in my life. But I didn't want to look beyond that. I just wanted to take it day by day. But that didn't work for her. We went out once more, but once again we had an even bigger argument about the same thing. Nancy wanted to know if I was dating her with a purpose in mind or just dating. I was honest. I told her I couldn't answer that yet. That night was the end of our relationship. She blames me. I blame her. Was I wrong?

Cast Your Vote on the Web

Now that you've chosen your ending, go to www.william-july.com and cast a vote for your choice. The results will be updated instantly, and you'll be able to see what others are thinking about our bachelor Rod.

A Final Note: Scientific Research on Bachelors

On June 26, 2002, Dr. David Popenoe and Dr. Barbara Dafoe Whitehead of the National Marriage Project at Rutgers University published the study "The State of Our Unions 2002: Why Men Won't Commit: Exploring Young Men's Attitudes About Sex, Dating, and Marriage." Of course, the study created a huge tumult when it hit the media. After talking to groups of single, never-married men in several cities, the researchers summarized their findings in the ten following points. Basically, they found that the men in the study avoided commitment because:

1. They can get sex without marriage more easily than in times past.

2. They can enjoy the benefits of having a wife by cohabiting rather than marrying.

3. They want to avoid divorce and its financial risks.

4. They want to wait until they are older to have children.

5. They fear that marriage will require too many changes and compromises.

6. They are waiting for the perfect soul mate and she hasn't appeared yet.

7. They face few social pressures to marry.

8. They are reluctant to marry a woman who already has children.

9. They want to own a house before they get a wife.

10. They want to enjoy single life as long as they can.

To many women seeking a mate for marriage or long-term committment, that information may have been disappointing, even somber. But is it all bad news? I think not. This study so intrigued me that I called the researchers. When I talked with them, they revealed an interesting ray of hope hidden among the interviews of the young single men and the statistics they'd compiled. It wasn't that the men in the study were totally opposed to marriage; rather, they had the listed reasons for avoiding marriage. On the surface that may sound like a minor detail. But actually it's a major direction sign that shows us where we need to go from here.

Relationships and marriage today are facing challenges and adjustments that didn't exist one hundred, fifty, or even twenty-five years ago. Things have changed drastically and will continue to change as the roles of men and women grow and adapt to ever-evolving new social postures. The ideas and feelings expressed by the men in the study are a snapshot of today's social climate. This is the climate in which we all will have to address the factors that create in men the reluctance to graduate from bachelor to groom. In other words, now we know where we are on the issue, and from here we can go where we all want to be: in happy, strong relationships. When viewed in that light, the findings of this study aren't a bitter end, but an exciting new beginning.

Does this mean no more traditional weddings with flowing white gowns, rice, and horse-drawn carriages? Of course not. People are naturally drawn to love, intimacy, and pairings for life. But how we get to that place is what we will have to create a new focus to understand. Brides-to-be, don't be discouraged and dismayed. Remember, the men in this study didn't say they never wanted to get married; but they're telling us lots of other things.

I encourage you to take a closer look at this study and read between the lines to identify the places we can move relationships and marriages forward from here. The authors of the study have done an excellent job of presenting their study in a nontechnical, user-friendly format. You can see the study online at http://marriage.rutgers.edu/TEXT-SOOU2002.htm. The main website for the National Marriage Project at Rutgers University is http://marriage.rutgers.edu/default.htm.

Books, Movies, and Websites on Bachelor-Related Issues

There is not a lot of written material specifically on the lives of bachelors. The following books, movies, and websites cover a mixed variety of issues concerning men. Please note that the mention of a book, website, or film here is not an endorsement, but is intended only to help you discover more information about bachelors, men, and relationships in general.

BOOKS FEATURING BACHELOR-RELATED ISSUES

Bonita Bennett, *How to Catch and Keep the Man of Your Dreams* (Harbon Publishing).

Stephen Carter and Julia Sokol, *He's Scared, She's Scared:*

Understanding the Hidden Fears That Sabotage Your Relationships (DTP).

——— , *Men Who Can't Love* (Berkley).

Cassandra Marshall Cato-Louis and Monique Jellerette deJongh, *How to Marry a Black Man* (Doubleday).

Barbara De Angelis, *What Women Want Men to Know* (Hyperion).

Ron Ellmore, *How to Love a Black Man* (Warner).

Marion P. Howard et al., *Men Who Never: Male Response to Women, Commitment and Marriage in the Culture of Today—Through the Testimony of 30 Life-Long Bachelors* (Pentland).

T. D. Jakes, *The Lady, Her Lover and Her Lord* (Berkley).

William July II, *Brothers, Lust, and Love* (Doubleday).

——— , *The Hidden Lover* (Broadway).

——— , *Understanding the Tin Man* (Doubleday).

Brenda Lane Richardson, *Guess Who's Coming to Dinner: Celebrating Interethnic, Interfaith and Interracial Relationships* (Wildcat Canyon Press).

Brenda Shoshanna, *Why Men Leave: Men Talk About Why They Decided to End the Relationship—And What Might Have Changed Their Minds* (Perigee).

Charles A. Waehler, *Bachelors* (Praeger).

Terry Watts, *Women Please Wake Up, Men Know What They Want* (VIM).

MOVIES WITH BACHELOR-RELATED ISSUES

A Cool Dry Place
Forces of Nature
Love and Basketball
She's Having a Baby
Swingers
What Women Want
When Harry Met Sally
The Wood

WEBSITES WITH BACHELOR-RELATED ISSUES

allaboutmen.com
A website featuring information, interviews, and topics about men.

askmen.com
A general variety of entertainment, issues, and information about men.

askheartbeat.com
General relationship advice with an African American and interethnic focus, including topics on male issues in relationships.

emale.com
A general variety of entertainment, issues, and information about men.

luvshades.com
General relationship advice with an African American focus, including topics on male issues in relationships.

mensjournal.com
This is the companion website of *Men's Journal* magazine, featuring a variety of issues about men.

tlcdiscovery.com (click on *A Wedding Story)*
This is the companion website for *A Wedding Story*, a television documentary series about how couples meet and marry.

About William July II

William July is a dynamic author and speaker who creates lively and entertaining dialogue while providing sage advice to readers and audiences. He creatively engages individuals and couples in constructive dialogue to promote healthy relationships and personal development. Though William holds a master's degree in psychology, he says his most important tool is providing "a dose of straightforward common sense."

William frequently appears on radio and television programs nationwide and in popular national magazines such as *Essence, Cosmopolitan, Jet, Ladies' Home Journal,* and *Redbook.* Critics have praised his books in *Publishers Weekly, New York Newsday,* Amazon.com, America Online, and numerous other media. In addition to being a writer and speaker, William is a professor of psychology. He is also pursuing his Ph.D. in Applied Social Psychology. William lives in Austin, Texas, with his wife, Jamey.

You can visit William July online at williamjuly.com

MARRIAGE Req AS HIGHER
FUNCTION of THINKING + CONDUC
BEHAVIOR

HE MUST OVERCOME BIOLOGICAL
DESIRES FOR THE GREATER GOOD.

~~HOW~~

① MONOGAMY
② MUST BE real, Relational. Free
PROBLEMS & ISSUES.
③ MUST CONTINUE TO GROW IN
Masculine Maturity, Spiritually